BUT I DIGRESS

There have been a few problems at home. Two weeks ago the man came round to re-cover the settee, and since then it's been incredibly lumpy. Added to which, we haven't seen my wife's mother for a fortnight, so it's very worrying. And on Tuesday there was another incident when I'd got up in the middle of the night to fix myself a snack – I went too near the extractor fan and ended up sailing through next door's bedroom window. As a matter of fact they've been a bit of a nuisance next door. A few weeks ago they bought this big new water bed, with a very powerful electric blanket on top. And at two o'clock every morning they both start whistling.

But I digress . . .

About the Author:

David Renwick has been writing comedy for radio
and television for nearly twenty years. Despite this
he is still extremely old. As well as writing
regularly for The Two Ronnies, he has worked
with many other comedians including Roy Hudd,
Harry Worth, Les Dawson, Bruce Forsyth, Mike
Yarwood, Spike Milligan and Kenny Everett.
Together with Andrew Marshall he has written
The Burkiss Way for radio, and for television End
of Part One, Whoops Apocalypse, The Steam
Video Company, Hot Metal and Alexei Sayle's
Stuff. He also co-wrote the feature film of Whoops
Apocalypse released in 1987.

He lives in Luton, much to everyone's surprise.

BUT I DIGRESS

David Renwick

With illustrations by Willie Rushton

NEW ENGLISH LIBRARY
Hodder and Stoughton

Copyright © 1989 by David Renwick
Illustrations copyright © 1989 by
William Rushton

First published in Great Britain in
1989 by New English Library
paperbacks

An NEL paperback original

Printed and bound in Great Britain
for Hodder and Stoughton
paperbacks, a division of Hodder
and Stoughton Ltd., Mill Road,
Dunton Green, Sevenoaks, Kent
TN13 2YA (Editorial Office: 47
Bedford Square, London WC1B 3DP)
by Richard Clay Ltd., Bungay,
Suffolk. Photoset by Rowland
Phototypesetting Ltd., Bury St
Edmunds, Suffolk.

British Library C.I.P.

Renwick, David, *1951–*
    But I digress.
    I. Title
828'.91407

    ISBN 0-450-50809-9

Introduction

I was working on at least three different radio series at the time, and any phone call was guaranteed to shatter my concentration and make me a very irritable person indeed.

On the other end was Peter Whitmore, producer of *The Two Ronnies*, wanting to know if I could write a story for Ronnie Corbett in the chair. For that matter he didn't care where I wrote it, so long as it was ready by the end of the week. The show would be taped in front of a live audience on Sunday evening, and they needed the script in by Friday morning at the latest.

Well it's not every day you're asked to have a go at one of the premier comedy spots on British television, so I snapped it up like a shot. What I didn't know then was that I would go on to write all of Ronnie's monologues on the show for the next ten years. It was 29th November 1977.

I won't lie and say that writing all those meandering tales was easy. Writing comedy is never easy. Let's be honest, it's an unbelievably hideous experience. You get up in the morning, come downstairs, stare into space like a zombie all day, then go to bed again. If you're lucky, during that time you'll have jotted down one or two really original funny lines. If you're *incredibly* lucky you'll still think they're original and funny when you read them back the next morning.

Even then you can't always tell. In 1980 I wrote one particular sketch and thought 'This is the most awful, contrived idea I've ever come up with – they'll never do it.'

1

So I tore it up and tossed it in the bin. The next day I was desperate, fished out the pieces, sellotaped them together and sent it in for the hell of it. It was called Mastermind, and involved Ronnie Corbett delivering all his answers one question late. And it turned out to be one of the most popular sketches they ever did.

In production terms, of course, Ronnie's chat spot was always the easiest thing to mount in the whole show. While some of the elaborate musical items would occupy hours of recording time the day before, 'RC's Mono' would breeze through in a matter of minutes. Down would come the black backcloth, the chair would be wheeled on from the wings, Ronnie would be given a leg-up by the floor manager, and away he'd go.

Of all the comedians I've worked with I can honestly say that Ronnie stands head and shoulders beneath the rest. But his comic skills and immaculate timing are, of course, pure joy. And when, like me, you take your comedy very seriously, working with someone who is a consummate analyst is an endlessly rewarding experience. Our conversations about work were always a delight: he was forever talking about the particular grammar and syntax of a joke, always self-aware and in control of his own technique.

He is the most un-vindictive of comedians, and never happier – or funnier – than when telling jokes against himself, and encouraging the audience to laugh at his own fictitious shortcomings and ineptitude.

For ten years I found myself being taken over by the character of Ronnie Corbett's rambling little man in the armchair. In fact I was telling my agent about it only the other day, and he was so surprised he almost dropped his tray of matches . . .

But I digress.

David Renwick

Do you want me to be funny . . . ?

Tonight I'd like, if I may, to tell you a brand new cricketing joke, which has never been heard before. Actually, when I say it's never been heard before that's not *entirely* true. Let's be honest, this joke is so old it was found buried with the Dead Sea Scrolls. As was the comedian who'd just told it. It dates back to 256 BC, which, as scholars of Ancient Egypt will know, was the year of the famous wildcat strike by the Amalgamated Union of Eunuchs and Allied Sopranos, in a dispute over severance pay. Incidentally, since the last show I'd like to thank all those of you who have written in with suggestions about what I can do with my act . . . and the one or two of you who sent diagrams. Offers of work have been flooding in: last week I was invited to go on a round-the-world cruise, by the chairman of the Flat Earth Society. And this week I was asked to do a very important after-dinner speech. I said 'Do you want me to be funny?' They said 'No, just be yourself.' It was actually a rather swish do, being held to commemorate fifty years of the BBC Canteen. And it was very moving – some of the original sausage rolls were there. Brought a lump to many throats. And it took me back to my own early career in the catering trade, when I was a lift boy on a dumb waiter. As I say, it was a very formal occasion. But somebody, for a joke, had told me it was fancy dress. So there we all are, the Director General, the Chairman of

3

the BBC, the governors, all standing around in their smart suits and dinner jackets . . . and I'm trying to act casual . . . dressed as Bo Beep . . . with my glass of sherry in one hand and my crook in the other. I remember thinking it was actually the first fancy dress party I'd been to since May 10th 1975. I remember it clearly because it was the day there wasn't a sale on at Allied Carpets. On that occasion I put on the tin legs from a suit of armour and went as a pair of nut-crackers. To be honest, it was the usual low-budget affair, this dinner. Hosted by a repeat of Terry Wogan. And it was four hours before the BBC Cheese Board arrived. *They* held a meeting and decided we couldn't have any cheese.

However, I seem to have wandered from the point. I was going to tell you this joke, about a small country cricket team that is in the doldrums. Now don't ask me which part of the doldrums, I think it was the northern part. I spent a couple of weeks there myself last summer, and that was a mistake from the word go. We were staying in a friend's cottage, and the heating system was a bit temperamental. When we got there it was snowing in the airing cupboard. The rising damp was so bad the mice were punting round on the mouse-traps. The doctor had told me to take a break because he said I'd been over-working. And I suppose I have been taking on rather a lot recently. I've been very active in our local pressure group, Short Comedians Against Bo Derek. Although to be honest I don't put a lot of faith in my doctor's judgment these days. My wife asked if he'd got something for a rather creaky hip joint, and he gave her two tickets to Ronnie Scott's.

But I digress. And back to the joke, about the local cricket team, who are going through a bit of a rough patch, needing an average of 97.3 runs an over to clinch the game . . . their top batsman can't see too well – during the interval he had to have a sight-screen to eat an orange – and the squad are currently without their main fast bowler while his wheelchair is being serviced, and not to put too fine a point on it the match is a slaughter. So after the game, the chairman decides he will put an advert in the local paper 'Bats-person wanted. Ability to hit the ball an advantage. Apply, blah blah blah blah blah, etc., etc.' Well a month goes by and there is no response of any kind. And the chairman thinks 'I wonder if I should have put our name and address, instead of blah blah blah blah blah, etc., etc.' Well it can make a difference. And just as he's thinking this, there is a knock on the door, and in walks a horse. And the horse casually pulls up a chair, sits down, lights a cigar, and says 'I understand you're looking for some new players. I wonder if I might put my services at your disposal.' The chairman says 'But you're a horse.' And the horse says 'I know.' Because it's not stupid. He says 'I'm rather nifty with the old willow, and the least you can do is give me a trial, old bean.'

So they go down to the nets, and sure enough the horse plays some strokes that make Viv Richards look like a fly swatter, and the chairman is so impressed he signs him up, and the following weekend the horse is put in as opening bat. Out it strides to the crease, in its shin-pads and its gloves, and its horse-box, and it is a sensation. In the first over it drives every delivery clean out of the stadium, six after six after six. And the club's regular supporters are astounded, and both have to be treated for shock. Then comes the second over; and the first ball, the other batsman plays a fluke hook-shot and starts racing up the pitch to snatch a quick single. But to his astonishment the horse doesn't move – it just stands there, motionless. And the batsman shouts 'What are you *doing*! Run! For God's sake! Run! Run!' And the horse says 'Run? Do me a favour – if I could run I'd be at bloody Epsom.'

Meanwhile, in Dagenham . . .

Tonight a rather interesting tale about a man who comes from Dagenham. Which is rather appropriate as I have recently moved out of a house in Dagenham. Well that place was too cramped for comfort. Every time the morning paper arrived I went flying out the back window. And I have to be honest, it was something of a rough area. We had to put a Krooklock on the cat. I remember once, the lady next door held a Tupperware Party and all police leave was cancelled. In fact the crime rate was so high there was a six-month waiting list to get mugged. Fortunately our new house in much nicer. I say new, actually its age and background are somewhat suspect. But all it needs is a spot of paint here and there, and once we get rid of the hunchback in the belfry it'll be as good as new. I have to admit the garden is a bit overgrown. My wife was hanging out some washing yesterday and three Japanese soldiers came out and surrendered. She was so frightened she ran away and hid behind the clothes prop. I forgot to tell you she's on a diet. That sounds ridiculous but my wife is incredibly self-conscious about her size. How many people do you know who would pay a speak-your-weight machine hush money? And at the moment she's incredibly thin. With her tongue out she looks like a zip. So on Saturday I decided to give her a hand with the housework, during which I accidentally fell into the tumble drier. My two young children came in and thought they were watching Magic Roundabout. Luckily I had my wits about me. I did three minutes of my cabaret act and they got up and switched off.

I was still a bit shaken the next day when I went up to see our producer in the Oval Office. As I walked in he was sitting behind his desk, arranging a bunch of pansies – for a special he's doing with the Osmond Brothers. Then he put the phone down and came over to me, sipping his glass of low-calorie meths. He stroked his chin for a moment, then stroked mine. He said 'What are you doing for your little chattie-poohs tonight luvvy?' I daren't do that voice too often, I might get to like it. I said I'm going to do the one about the chap from Dagenham, which I happened to overhear in the canteen. I don't go up to the canteen much these days but today was a special occasion. They were presenting one of the steak and kidney pies with a gold watch. And two fellows nearby were talking. One of them was a producer with BBC Scotland. The last I heard he was due to make a new series all about the Arts in Glasgow, called 'Stitch *that*, Jimmy!' But it never came off. The story goes that he annoyed Paul Daniels in the bar one day and spent three weeks inside a matchbox.

Anyway, this was the joke they were telling. About the chap from Dagenham. Now don't ask me why he came from Dagenham. There's nowt as queer as folk. As I remember my Uncle Doris telling me, shortly before he was cashiered from the Wrens. The important thing is that he's flying this plane on a solo flight around the world. Next to which the Dagenham bit is pretty irrelevant, so I don't know why I bothered to mention it. So off he goes on this solo flight in his lightweight Moulinex turbo-prop, and as luck would have it a freak wind blows him off course and he has to make a forced landing slap-bang in the middle of the African jungle. 'Blow it!' he says. Or a word to that effect. 'Now I'm stranded. No food, no water supplies; thank God I brought some luncheon vouchers.' Suddenly, at that moment there is a rustle in the bushes, and from out of the undergrowth steps this seven-foot tall African native: bone through the nose, shrunken heads hanging round his neck. I think *he* was from Dagenham actually. And carrying in his hand a rude spear. Which we won't dwell on. Well naturally the chap is just about to start saying his prayers, when the native speaks to him, he says 'Pardon me my good man, but I – (*whistle*) – can't help noticing that you – (*whistle*) – seem to be in some distress. I was therefore – (*whistle*) – wondering if I might perchance be of any – (*whistle*) – assistance to you.' The chap says 'Well that's very kind.' He says 'Not at all, sir, I'm only too – (*whistle*) – happy to co-operate in whatever – (*whistle*) – way you desire.' Well at this point the chap's curiosity gets the better of him, he says 'Look, excuse me for asking, but here we are in the middle of the jungle – how is it you can speak such immaculate English?' And the native says 'Well as a matter of fact, I – (*whistle*) – picked it up on short-wave radio.'

This little piggy had a wooden leg

Now the joke I'm going to tell you tonight is not exactly the funniest joke in the world. I'll be honest, this joke is so unfunny, I told it to Stuart Hall of *It's a Knockout* and he only laughed for two and half hours. We were in the BBC Club at the time, and things were a bit boisterous. One of Paul Daniels' tricks had got out of hand and there were seventy-three Nolan Sisters at the bar. And over in the corner people were agog with the news that Patrick Moore's suit had just walked into a dry cleaner's and given itself up. Because he's had a lot of trouble with that suit – the moths in his jacket have just applied for a home improvement grant. And as usual our producer was feeling a bit full of himself – as he stood there with a pint of Guinness between his legs, trying to get the froth out with a corkscrew. Oh by the way, I forgot. A little wave to my wife . . . who, to be honest, has not been herself just lately, not since I got her that part-time job, as a lollipop lady at Brands Hatch. No, let's face it, there have been a few problems at home recently – that episode with the settee in the front room. Two weeks ago the man came round to re-cover it, and since then it's been *incredibly* lumpy. Added to which, we haven't seen my wife's mother for a fortnight, so it's very worrying. And on Tuesday there was another incident when I'd got up in the middle of the night to fix myself a snack – I went too near the extractor fan and

11

ended up sailing through next door's bedroom window. That took the wind out of their sails I can tell you. As a matter of fact they've been a bit of a nuisance next door. A few weeks ago they bought this big new water bed, with a very powerful electric blanket on top. And at two o'clock every morning they both start whistling. And of course I've had a lot of worries myself, ever since I bought that racehorse from Tesco's. Now I know that sounds ridiculous, doesn't it. How could anyone be so stupid as to buy a racehorse from Tesco's? But I did. I got 5p off because it had a dent in it. No I didn't really buy a racehorse from Tesco's. I actually bought a zebra. I thought it was a racehorse with a bar code on it.

But I digress. And on to the story, which all takes place on a farm, where one day this chap turns up to do a spot of casual work, and is given the job of cleaning out the pigsties. Incidentally, if at any point you are dazzled by my fluent grasp of agricultural terms, like 'pig' and 'sty', I should point out that I did once work on a farm myself. A very small farm to be honest. We had one sheep, and that was seventy-five per cent polyester. As it happened I only worked on this farm for a few weeks – I used to take the cockerel round every night to charge up the battery hens. And it wasn't easy because they'd just formed a vigilante group to hunt down Colonel Sanders. That was at night time. In the day time I was told to go out and cut the corn. Nothing changes. So there's this chap, happily hoovering out the pigsties, when suddenly he notices that one of the pigs has got a wooden leg. Now don't ask me which pig it was. For the sake of argument we'll call it Bernard. Bernard Manning. No we won't . . . be unfair to the pig like that. So, full of curiosity, he immediately takes it to the farmer and he says 'I hope you'll excuse me asking this, but I can't help noticing that this pig has got a wooden leg. Why would this be, pray?' And the farmer says 'If it wasn't for that pig, this farm wouldn't be here. A few weeks ago when I was away on holiday, a fire broke out in that hayloft. Straight away, that pig smelt the smoke, jumped out of the

12

sty, raced over to that shed, got out the hose-pipe, connected it to that tap there, and then turned on the water and put out all the flames. And then rang the local fire brigade to come over and clean up the mess. If it hadn't been for that pig the whole place would have gone up in smoke.' The chap says 'That's absolutely incredible, for a pig to do a thing like that, but why has it got a wooden leg?' The farmer says 'And I'll tell you another thing. That pig saved my life. Two weeks ago I was in town on business, and two muggers cornered me in an alleyway and pulled a gun. So I shouts for help, and from five miles away the pig hears me, jumps out of the sty, leaps onto a bicycle and cycles all the way into town, then with two swift karate chops from its trotter, fells both the muggers and immediately disarms them. Then, seeing I've fainted, it gives me the kiss of life, and carries me on its back to the nearest doctor for assistance. If it wasn't for that pig I wouldn't be alive today.' So the chap, once again, says 'That's the most amazing story I've ever heard. But I've got to know this – why has it got a wooden leg?' The farmer says 'Listen – when you've got a pig like that, you don't eat it all at once.'

Clarence the Unlucky

Here is a joke which my dear little grey-haired old mother used to tell me many years ago. Whenever I had trouble getting off to sleep. Unlike tonight, when I'm having trouble staying awake. That, obviously, will give you some idea of how riveting tonight's joke is. I'll be honest, this story has all the excitement of an overdose of Horlicks. As usual it's not entirely new, in fact the history books show this joke was a big favourite at the court of King Henry the Eighth. When you think of it, times haven't changed much. In those days if you told bad jokes you ended up on the chopping block. Today it's *Celebrity Squares*. Though come to think of it, one pain in the neck's much the same as another. I'm surprised my mother told me this joke because I had a very strict upbringing. My rude awakening to the seamier side of life didn't come till one night when I was round at a girl's house playing a game of chess. She'd got one of her pawns to my end of the board and I asked her if she wanted to make a knight of it. We never played a lot of chess after that. And of course I did live in a very religious community. Where we lived the local Catholic Church had to board up the confessional box. Every Sunday evening we used to gather in the church and pray for wicked women. You've guessed, none of them ever showed up. I'll never forget the day the town's Mormon missionary came round everyone's door and said 'Oi, my life . . . !' Sometimes I don't think his heart was in his job. 'Oi! My life,' he said. I should point out he was actually half Mormon and half Jewish. His parents came from Salt Beef City. 'My life,' he said, 'the world is going to end at 6.35 next Tuesday!' And everybody took it so seriously, the Catholics organised a last-minute mass, the Anglicans arranged emergency communion and the local synagogue held a closing-down sale.

But back to the joke, which is all about a rather unlucky man who is called up to join the navy. And before he goes his mother says to him 'Clarence,' she says. I told you he was unlucky. 'Clarence, whatever you do, don't forget to write and let me know how you're getting on.' So off Clarence goes to war, and he's a little bit nervous at first, about getting killed and how it will affect his health. Well we all have to be careful. By rights I shouldn't really be here tonight. Only last week my doctor told me 'If you do any more of those long stories in that chair,' he said, 'you're soon going to get run down.' I said 'Rubbish.' He said 'You are if you come near *my* car.' I'd actually gone to see him with my nose, and . . . well I didn't actually *see* him with my nose. That would be ridiculous. I actually saw him with my eyes. But I had my nose on me at the time. I was feeling a bit sniffly, so he gave me this jar of incredibly strong vapour rub. I said 'Will it clear my nose?' He said 'It'll probably clear the studio.'

Back to Clarence, who has now settled down to naval life, and after he's been away for a few months his mother receives this letter from him which says 'Dear Mummy. Because of censorship regulations I cannot tell you where-abouts in the world I am. But yesterday we had shore leave and I shot a polar bear. Love, Clarence.' So all appears to be OK, a few weeks go by, and she gets another letter. 'Dear Mummy. I still cannot tell you which part of the world I am in, but we went ashore again yesterday and I danced with a hula hula girl. Your loving son, Clarence.' So once again all's fine, until a couple of weeks later she gets a third letter which reads 'Dear Mummy. I still cannot tell you exactly where I am. But the ship's medical officer visited me today – and said it would have been better if I'd danced with the polar bear and shot the hula hula girl.'

Why I'm big in Ireland

My story tonight concerns an Irishman who is not terribly bright. Now I don't want to imply that all Irishmen are not terribly bright, because I happen to be very big in Ireland. Among the Little People I am very big. In fact over there a lot of folk think I *am* one of the Little People. I remember a few years ago when I was in Ireland on holiday, I went out for a little walk in the country, and I'd just sat down in this cow field, which was rather apt because it was Pancake Tuesday, and a woman who was passing by noticed me, and insisted on taking me home for the night. Because she said I was lucky. As it turned out I *was* pretty lucky, but that's another story. Which I'm not telling *you*.

Sometimes being small can have its advantages, sometimes it can be very embarrassing. When I first left school, for a time I did a bit of work as a male model. I used to pose for the centre pages of slightly racy magazines. Like *Shorthouse* and *Flour Graders Only*. Usually wearing nothing except a little bowler hat, displaying all that nature had given me. I've never received so many get well cards in my life. It's very hard to believe, but in those days I was incredibly weedy. Everywhere I went people kept laughing at me. I wish they were in the audience tonight. So I decided to take one of those body building courses. It was quite good; they sent me one of those little contraptions where you sit and exercise your feet on the pedals but it never actually moves from the spot. An Austin 1100. I also

19

bought myself a set of chest expanders, but my wife started practising with them and she overdid it. I used to lie next to her in bed and I couldn't see the alarm clock.

Where was I? I seem to have strayed from the point, which won't please the director, because he's obsessed with this fear of the show over-running. Sometimes he lies awake at rehearsals worrying about it. And he's not very happy with me this week because he didn't want me to tell this particular joke. On Wednesday I got the Royal Summons to his office, and as I opened the door and stepped over his secretary I could see I'd picked a bad moment. He said 'Ah Corbett, why don't you tell them that awfully funny joke, about the shellfish.' I said 'I'm sorry I don't know any jokes about shellfish.' He said 'Yes you do, the one about the sex-mad cockle, who goes out every Saturday night and pulls a mussel.' I said 'I happen to think that's absolutely pathetic. The one I've got is a lot funnier.' He said 'All right, there's no need to boast.' No need to boast! Coming from the man who every night walks into the BBC bar and shouts 'Mine's a large one!', I thought that was pretty rich.

Anyway, onwards very quickly. There is this jumbo jet, flying through the night across the Atlantic to London. And all the passengers are sitting comfortably in the first-class compartment waiting for the joke to begin. When suddenly a voice comes over the intercom (*holds his nose*) 'Your attention please. This is your captain speaking . . .' Actually, *he* didn't hold his nose like that when he spoke. I just did that to add a touch of realism. 'Your attention please. We are cruising at an altitude of approximately 35,000 feet above the Atlantic, at an average speed of 564 miles an hour and number one engine has just fallen off. As a result we shall now be about twenty minutes late at Heathrow.' Well the passengers all took the news fairly calmly, and then a few minutes later, on he comes again. 'Your attention please, I'm afraid we now have lost number two engine. This means we shall be about forty minutes late arriving in London.' Well, another half hour goes by and then the intercom is switched on again. 'Your attention please. We have now lost number three engine, and I'm afraid we're going to be a couple of hours late on this run.' Well, an ominous silence descends over all the passengers and then up pipes a little Irishman sitting in the corner: 'Let's hope they don't lose any more engines, or we'll be up here all night.'

'I thought the earwig had a good game . . .'

The joke I'm about to tell you tonight, I can say with complete confidence, is rather priceless. I can say that because we had it valued by Arthur Negus before we came on. He put it at early sixteenth century and possibly one of a pair. The other one is Frank Carson's act. No that's not true. I'll be honest, this joke was actually told to me just after lunch today by our producer, as he was being carried down from the bar. Incidentally I'm not going to make any unkind remarks about our producer drinking, because I don't think you should mock a man's religion. And besides he does have a sad family history – his father used to suffer from a lot of hangovers so they put him on a course of Alka Seltzer tablets for seven years, and one day he dissolved in the bath.

Having been told this joke at short notice I haven't had time to try it out on the camera crew. It's a BBC rule that before you're allowed to do a story on TV you have to tell it first of all to the cameramen. And if they laugh you have to go away and clean it up. Anyway this story is a football story actually, which will appeal to soccer enthusiasts and Fulham supporters alike. And it concerns . . . excuse me, I'm a bit frightened this chair may give way under my weight. As a matter of fact I went to see the Head of Comedy about it, and . . . They *call* him the Head of Comedy . . . He's a man who sits behind a desk all day with

23

a false nose on. And once a month he calls all the top producers into his office to watch his bow-tie spin round. So I went to see him; he said 'Archie –' I forgot to tell you, he still thinks I'm Archie Andrews. It was a little white lie I had to tell him after last year's Christmas party, when he caught me sitting on his secretary's knee with her hand up the back of my shirt. 'Archie,' he said, 'if you want a new chair you'll have to put in a claim to the Director General.' So I did what he said, I wrote to the Director General about the chair being cracked, and immediately he snapped into action, and sent me a tube of glue. Together with this note, which reads 'Dear Mr Corbett. Re your complaint about a cracked chair. Please contact our props department and they'll be pleased to tell you where to stick it.'

So back to the story, which all takes place in the jungle, where a bunch of insects and a few of their friends have challenged the elephants to a game of football. And everyone's come along to watch: the local cannibals are all sitting there on the touchline eating their portions of Kentucky Fried Missionary, and the gorillas are all lumbering around with scarves tied to their wrists; and out come the two teams, the elephants and the insects, and the match begins. Now it's a bit of a dirty game, because after only twenty minutes the elephants have been booked for fouling three players, two spectators and 75 per cent of the pitch. And the insects can't seem to find their form at all. They've all been out the night before sampling the local talent, chatting up loose cockroaches, and having a naughty time at a bee-hive of ill repute, where they got stung for ten quid a time. So they can't get it together at all, and by half time the elephants are leading 146–nil. Then, at the start of the second half, the insects make a substitution. They take off a rather slow moth at left-wing, and put in a centipede. Well the match begins again and after a few minutes the insects are awarded a free kick. The elephants are all standing there bunched up together in the defensive wall with their trunks between their legs, and the centipede takes the kick and slices the ball right through into the back of the net.

Well from then on the tide completely turns. The centipede keeps scoring and scoring and all the other insects go mad, cheering and clapping their mandibles together and wiping the tears from their eyes. The final whistle goes and the insects have won by 630 goals to 146.

Afterwards in the changing rooms the elephant captain comes over to the bluebottle who's captain of the insects and says 'What I still can't understand is, why didn't you play that centipede right from the start of the match?' The bluebottle says 'Well we would have done, but it takes him an hour and a half to get his boots on.'

By way of a special request . . .

Here is a very funny joke about a man who has lived all his life in Bradford. Quite funny so far isn't it? By the way, talking of Bradford, this is not the joke about the Indian gentleman who always slept on a bed of nails and divorced his wife because she refused to get down to brass tacks. I wish it had been that joke actually, it's a damn sight funnier than the one I'm going to tell you. However the reason I'm going to tell you this one is because I've had a special request. Normally I don't do a lot of viewers' requests. Let's face it, 90 per cent of them are physically impossible, but this one is from my wife and I'm hoping it will buck her up because she's been a bit under the weather, and to be honest I think it's affecting her eyesight. Last Wednesday she spent half an hour telling our garden gnome his tea was ready. It's strange but in all the years we've been married this joke is one of the two things that have really made my wife laugh. And you're wrong about the other one. Actually things have been a wee bit tense on the domestic front recently. It all started last weekend. I'd just popped round to visit our local. But unfortunately she was out, so I went down the pub. One of those quaint old rural places. At one time when you went in it used to be full of country atmosphere, then the landlord put up a sign saying 'Please wipe your feet.' On this occasion they were holding their weekly Yard of Ale contest. Everybody in the pub drinks six pints of ale, then dashes out into the yard. Well, when I got home I found my wife in tears because the

27

gas stove had blown up. It was one of those rather dangerous old Japanese models, with the suicide pilot. She'd been on at me for ages to get her a new one. She used to keep dropping subtle little hints; like she'd come back from the Indian takeaway and ram a chicken vindalou down my trousers. And very nearly curried my favour, I can tell you. She claims I'm lazy and I suppose I am lazy, it's something I inherited from my mother. When I was a little boy, on bath nights, she couldn't be bothered to rub a towel over my legs, she used to stand me in the spin drier. For seven years I had to screw my trousers on. My brothers and sisters kept coming up saying 'Now *there's* a twist.'

However I'm starting to ramble again, and I mustn't because the producer did ask me to be brief as he wants to get away early. Probably another of his council meetings. He serves on this local council, and by all accounts did extremely well at the last election by managing to hold on to his seat in a Gay Lib stronghold.

But back to the chap, who is still living in Bradford, and understandably getting a bit fed up with it by now. So he decides to go on a cruise to the West Indies. Actually this is the same man, you know, as in the other joke, whose *wife* kept going to the West Indies, and he's had enough of being left behind all the while, so he's going out to see what it's like for himself. So he boards the ship at Plymouth, hands in his little ticket, and is led down some creaking old steps into the ship's hold. And there he sees all the passengers are sitting chained to great wooden oars. Row upon row of haggard, perspiring bodies all heaving together. Just like a British Rail ferry really. Actually it reminds me more of a rickety old troop ship I was put on during the war. An utter disgrace, but I remember there was one spot of good news, owing to a shortage of space all the soldiers had to share sleeping quarters with the Wrens. The bad news was they slept in hammocks. You've never seen a boat rock about so much in all your life . . .

So the chap's sitting there all chained up behind his oar, and the order's given and they all start rowing. And right at the end there's a man with a huge drum, beating out this relentless rhythm for them to keep time to. BOOM-*BOOM*! . . . BOOM-*BOOM*! . . . BOOM-*BOOM*! . . . Sounds like Basil Brush at half speed . . . BOOM-*BOOM*! . . . Let me know if you start getting sea sick. And in these terrible inhuman conditions they row until they can row no more, and they reach the Caribbean, and a man comes round to undo their chains. And the chap staggers to his feet, clothes in shreds, his throat dry and cracked, picks up his suitcases, and starts to climb out. Then half way up the steps he turns back to the bloke who was sitting next to him, and says 'Just a minute. Do you think we ought to tip the drummer?' And the other bloke says 'No, I shouldn't think so. I didn't bother last year.'

Laugh? Well what if they didn't?

Tonight, instead of a joke, I'd like to relate a rather amusing incident that happened a couple of days ago. In fact I was telling it to the other members of the cast here just before we came on. Ha ha ha . . . laugh? Well what if they didn't? It was understandable really because most of us here are a little bit upset over a nasty accident that took place this afternoon in the next studio. It was during rehearsals for one of those big variety shows. This acrobat had put on a pair of close-fitting tights and was doing a rather novel balancing act. He was straddling a couple of high chairs, wondering whether or not to try and do the splits when suddenly they both collapsed underneath him. And he was torn between two stools. Very tragic, especially for his wife, who's now trying to pick up the pieces. It's symptomatic in a way of how everything's falling into disrepair here at the BBC. Like this old seat I have to sit on, it gets more uncomfortable every week. I told the producer this morning I'd had enough. I said 'There's an awkward little lump in this chair.' He said 'Don't I know it.' I said 'There's no need for wit, that's not like you at all. The solution is simple, the cushion needs stuffing.' And his reply is in the hands of my solicitor.

However, I shouldn't go on about our internal problems because tonight being the last of the series we've got the controller of BBC 1 in the audience. Come along for the free drinks afterwards I suppose. I'm not going to tell you whereabouts the controller is sitting. I won't mention the balding head or the smell of the ready-rubbed Condor. Because she's awfully sensitive about it. No that's not true, that's just a bit of comedy I put in. The controller is in fact a highly distinguished and important gentleman. Or so he keeps telling us. The reason I mustn't point him out is because he's sitting with his secretary and she is a little shy. With coconuts to match. As a matter of fact I've known our controller for a long time now because when he was Head of Comedy he was the one who first put forward the idea for this show: '*The Two Ronnies* – starring Ronnie Barker and Norman Wisdom.' Well everyone could see it wasn't *quite* right, so they held a big meeting of all the top comedy producers – the cream of the BBC plus one or two old yoghurts – and eventually my name came up as a replacement. '*The Two Ronnies*, starring Ronnie Corbett and Norman Wisdom.' It was all very flattering because at the time I was completely unknown, I didn't even recognise my face in the mirror. And work was thin on the ground. Around that time I was trying to earn a crust as a smalltime male stripper. I used to do very cheap hen parties. After they'd had all their food and drinks, at the climax of the evening I used to leap out of a sausage roll. And then slowly strip down to my thermal underwear. It was quite erotic actually. A lot of women used to jump onto the stage and feel my muscles. The rest used to jump up and feel my pulse.

However that is really by the way and nothing to do with the incident I set out to tell you about. Which occurred the other night in our local Jewish pub the Kosher Horses. I'd actually gone there more for business than pleasure, because I was attending a sort of union meeting, the Surrey branch of the Amalgamated Union of Pint-sized Comedians and Allied Midgets. And all the pint-sized comedians were present: Charlie Drake, Syd Little, David Steel. Then suddenly in the middle of the meeting a chap walked into the pub carrying a crocodile. And as I watched he went up to the bar and said 'Excuse me, do you serve Scotsmen in this hostelry?' The barman said 'Certainly'. He

32

said 'Well, give me a pint of beer and two Scotsmen for the crocodile.' Well, the barman, not wanting to cause a scene, pulled a pint of beer and handed over two Scotsmen who were sitting in the corner, whereupon the crocodile promptly ate them up. Fifteen minutes went by and the chap came up and ordered again: 'Pint of beer and two Scotsmen for the crocodile.' So once again the barman gave him a beer, called over two more Scotsmen, who were in the other bar wringing out their beer mats into a glass; and again the crocodile gobbled them up. Well, this went on for another hour or so until finally the chap came back again and said 'Same again, pint of beer and two Scotsmen for the crocodile.' The barman said 'Look, I'm very sorry, but we're clean out of Scotsmen. We've got none left, he's eaten them all.' And then to my horror his eyes travelled up the bar to where my party were sitting, and he said 'I tell you what, though, we haven't got any Scotsmen, but do you think he'd fancy Charlie Drake, Syd Little and Ronnie Corbett?' The chap said 'Ssshhh! For God's sake, whatever you do, don't start him on the shorts.'

'Just remember to pick your nose'

Tonight, I'd like to tell you the . . . excuse me. I'm sorry about that, but I can still feel my heart beating away here. I had a frightening experience tonight while crossing the road outside the studio. I was just stepping off the kerb and my parachute failed to open. Let's face it, this road here outside the television centre can be incredibly dangerous. A few years ago we all got a nasty shock when we heard that a black and white minstrel had been run over by a steamroller. For three days we'd all been using him as a zebra crossing. And I must try to stick to the point tonight because it keeps the producer happy. And no one wants to make life difficult as he's still quite new to the show . . . I don't want to talk too loudly in case I wake him up. He's actually very good, apart from this shocking memory. This afternoon he came up to me and said 'Excuse me, are you the fat one or the little one?' As he stood there in front of me, running the Black and Decker over his moustache, he said 'What joke are you bringing out of retirement *this* week?' I said 'I was thinking of doing the one about the zoo.' He said 'That's not the one about the Irish zoo-keeper who kept watering the bird seed is it? Or the one about the cow that has a night of fun with a wart-hog and ends up six months repugnant?' I said no, to be honest this particular joke is one I heard recently at one of those posh dinners.

The National Union of Undertakers' Annual Ball. They invite me along each year to crack a few jokes and boost trade. Although for me, doing after-dinner speeches can prove harrowing. If I stand still for too long the toastmaster starts banging my head on the table. And I've never got over an embarrassing experience a few years back when I received an invitation to a dinner which said 'Dress Optional'. And yes, you've guessed, when I turned up I found none of the other men was wearing one.

But back to the joke. And it's about this zoo which is rather short of animals. And to cap it all, their star attraction Des the Gorilla has just handed in his notice. Then one of the keepers says 'Why don't we get someone to dress up as a gorilla instead? All we need is someone who can lumber around a bit, suck a few bananas and scratch their armpits.' So they put an advert in the local press and the following day this fellow turns up; he says 'I don't normally do a lot of gorilla work. But times are hard. I've just been laid off at the Golders Green Bacon Company, and I need the money.' So they dress him up in the gorilla skin and stick him in the cage. And he's a bit nervous because he knows they're all out there; the Mums, the Dads, the kiddies, and his agent. So at first he plays it a bit low key and just sort of peeps out from behind the tree every fifteen minutes and picks his nose. And immediately the crowd go wild. 'More!' they shout, and 'Bravo!' And 'Eat your heart out, Bernard Manning!' And at this the chap starts gaining confidence, and he comes right out and really gets into the part, scraping his knuckles along the floor, beating his hands on his chest, generally hurting himself. And doing all the noises. 'Ooo! Ooo! Ooo!' Not quite as good as that, obviously, because he hadn't had my acting experience. And he gets so carried away he swings about on the rope and flies right over the cage wall and lands slap bang in the middle of the lions' den. And you can see the fear come over his face. Like a tomcat that's just seen the vet's car drawing up. And straightaway he's shouting 'Let me out! Let me out!' And rattling the bars, screaming his head off and really raising the roof. One of the lions stalks slowly up to him and says 'Look why don't you shut up – you'll get us *all* the sack.'

There was a young lady from Romford

(*Ronnie is surrounded by six other short men, all wearing identical sweaters and glasses.*)

Thank you very much. Before we begin tonight I've been asked to announce that following eleventh hour, top-level discussions between the BBC and Equity, the dispute over manning levels on the Ronnie Corbett Chair Spot has now been settled. Not to *everyone's* satisfaction, I would point out. But under the new union agreement there must be a minimum of seven Ronnie Corbetts present on the set at all times. One, who is funny and tells the joke, and the other six on stand-by. So now, on with tonight's joke.

(*One of the other Ronnie Corbetts now begins speaking.*)

Ronnie 2: Yes and it concerns a young lady from Romford, who is, one day, taking a walk through the country when she meets this farmer. Incidentally, stop me if you've heard this joke before, because it's a very –

Yes I *have* heard it! And she wasn't from Romford, she was from Ilford, you've made a complete mockery of the whole thing. Now go on, clear off the lot of you! I shall take my case to ACAS. It looked ridiculous anyway. Hands up all those who were expecting Snow White to come on? No, actually all that was just a piece of Christmas merriment. And talking of Christmas, I have just received this wonderful Christmas card from my wife. God knows how she found out the address. Now I don't know why I should say that because as a matter of fact we all had a fun-filled party at home last night. All the little wee Corbetts celebrating – pulling the cracker, with me as the anchor man.

This year I was up in Scotland, racing my new yacht. I've just bought this new yacht and I was racing it. Not very far – just up to the hot water tap and back again. Pathetic isn't it? A grown man – almost – still playing with toy boats in the bath. Well let's face it I've got precious little else to play with. Not since my rubber duck flew south for the winter. And I've actually been feeling a bit drained just lately – too many late nights, I suppose, with all the old show business cronies – the Roland Rat-pack. And we have had a lot of problems at home with all those household pests. Several days just lately my wife's come home to find me backing out of the mousehole with a chair and a whip.

This year work has been a bit thin on the ground. The other night I was having dinner with a hologram of my agent and I said to him 'Work has been a bit thin on the ground.' I said 'Look at what you've got me so far this year – two guest appearances on Trumpton – and compere at an autopsy.' And a rather unfortunate charity fete last summer, held as part of the relief effort for the victims of airline lunches. I'd been asked to perform a little ceremony with Barbara Windsor. And that's where it all went wrong, when I closed my eyes for the lucky dip . . .

Fortunately we're going off on a bit of a holiday after Christmas, my wife and I, and I just hope it's more successful than last time. Owing to a mix-up in the flight arrangements I spent six weeks playing Peter Pan at Wimbledon.

However, on with tonight's story, which I have promised to tell as a special request for all the folk at our local old people's home. Quite a boisterous crowd for their age. Last week there were twenty-seven arrests after spectators invaded the Ludo board. In fact it's such a rough place, it was the first old people's home to bring in the short, sharp shock for offenders. If one of the residents misbehaves they wire up his hearing-aid to a Kenwood blender. I know one old chap who stood still for too long in the garden and had his walking frame clamped. Well you have to be strict with the way crime is soaring these days. Where I live they've just arrested an Indian Rubber Man for stealing car radios through the exhaust pipe.

But I digress, and on with the story. And it's a rather interesting story about a rather prim and starchy lady – a bit of a blue stocking, or it might have been varicose veins, we're not sure. And she's walking along a country lane when she espies, coming towards her, a rather brawny, rough-looking man, leading a goat on a piece of string, carrying a chicken under one arm, a pig under the other, and balancing a bucket on his head. Well, the chap gets near her and he says 'Excuse me, but could you direct me to the Frog and Filofax public house, which I believe is near here?' She says 'Yes certainly. It's in front of the village duck pond. Just go down this road for about five miles, and when you feel your neck getting wet you'll know you've passed it.' She said 'There is a much quicker short cut through the woods but it's very complicated.' He said 'Oh dear, I'm not very good with complicated things, is there any chance you could take me there yourself?' The lady says 'What? Through the wood, with you – on my own? You could take advantage of me!' 'Oh come on,' the chap says, 'look at me – I've got a goat on a lead, a chicken under one arm, a pig under the other, and I'm balancing a bucket on my head. How on earth am I going to take advantage of you?' She said 'Well, you could tie the goat to a tree, stick the chicken under the bucket, and *I* could hold the pig.'

I can't see any future in clairvoyance

Tonight by way of a change I'd like to open by dipping into the mountain of fan mail which has arrived following last week's joke. Just a selection from the vast sacks of post and telegrams of congratulations that have been flooding in all week long. Let's be honest, I've had one letter. Why should I lie to you? I won't try and hide the fact that I never, ever get fan letters. The last time anyone had anything good to say about me was the drama critic of the *Times Literary Supplement*, who said that I was pushing back the barriers of comedy and reaching new, unexplored areas of humour. I think the actual words were 'Ronnie Corbett's getting beyond a joke.' But it was the same thing. All of which makes it so exciting that I've received this letter, only this morning, and I haven't even had time to open it yet. I just hope it says something nice. (*Opens the letter.*) 'Dear Ronnie. Just a note to thank you for the endless amusement you have always given me. Last Saturday night was the funniest yet, I still haven't stopped laughing. My husband will be away again this weekend too, so if you –' (*Hastily thrusts it away.*) Sorry about that; it was just the gas bill.

On to tonight's joke instead. Now I had a bit of a last minute panic over this one actually, because what happened was I went up to the canteen at lunchtime and it was all a bit quiet, because they were just holding a mass for the

43

trifle. And as usual the place was pretty deserted. I'll be honest, the BBC Canteen has seen better days. These days they're having to resort to cheap gimmicks to drum up trade. You can imagine our reaction last week when they announced they were going completely topless. Hurray, we said. No more crusts on the pies. In fact I was going to open a restaurant with topless waitresses myself once but I was put off by the enormous overheads. Then there was their other idea, three curries for the price of one, so you get a good run for your money. But that had no takers either. And as I entered I noticed, over at the corner table, our producer. I think he must have accidentally sobered up at that moment because he came over, fixed me through the old double-glazed eyes, and said 'What rave from the grave are you planning to thrill us with tonight?' I said 'If it's all right with you I'm going to do the one about the man whose bedroom catches fire. And the insurance company refuse to pay up because they maintain he actually came home that night as pickled as a beetroot – in fact his blood sample taken the next day had a head on it – and they're convinced he went to bed still smoking a cigarette and started the fire himself. To which the man replies that it's a pack of lies. "In the first place," he says, "I was stone cold sober when I came home, and in the second place the bed was already on fire when I got into it."' Now unfortunately our producer didn't care for that one much. To be honest I don't think he understood it. So I said I'd try and find another one, and I got on to my agents, Son and Goldberg. They're quite good but they know nothing about billing. I've been with them a long time now; in fact they got me my first job back in 1952, when I was offered a key part in the Hunchback of Notre Dame after a cushion dropped out at the last moment. Anyway as usual my agent came up with a goodie, about this chap who is very interested in psychic phenomena. You know the kind of thing, like when one day you suddenly hear from a person who died over twenty years ago. A bit like second-class post. And he happens to hear that up in Scotland there is an old man who is a psychic expert and can

44

read people's minds, so he goes up to the Scottish Highlands, and . . . Actually it's all rather nice that this happens in the Scottish Highlands. Because at least if you don't find the joke funny you can always admire the scenery. So he calls round at the house of this weirdo with the psychic powers and he knocks on the door and says to the maid, 'Excuse me, but I understand the gentleman who lives here is possessed of incredible gifts of clairvoyance, can read people's minds, see into the future, and generally is able to foresee everything that's about to happen in the entire world.' She said 'That's perfectly correct – is he expecting you?' Well to cut a long story not quite so short he goes in and meets this wizened little man who says to him 'Och aye, for five hundred poonds I will teach you everything I know about telepathy,' and he takes him outside into the garden, brings out a hose-pipe and fixes it onto the tap. He says 'Just take hold of the other end of this, hold it up to your eye and have a look down inside it.' The chaps says 'What's this all got to do with mind reading?' The man says 'Just do as I say.' So he holds up the end of the hose to his eye, and stands there squinting down inside it, and immediately the old man turns on the tap and, whooosh! right in the eye. And the chap is drenched to the skin, he hurls the hose-pipe down in disgust, storms over to the old man and says 'I knew damn well you were going to do that!' The old man says 'There you are, you see, we're half way there already.'

And now the bad news . . .

Tonight a slight change of policy, I'm going to tell a new joke. In fact this joke is so new I haven't even heard it myself yet. Well, it's been a very busy and somewhat distressing week at home. Some scaremonger down our road had been putting a story about that his son had joined the local Tufty Club and gone down with myxomatosis. All of which upset our little boy, who was already in tears over the news that the new train set we'd bought him for his birthday had been cancelled due to staff shortages. So by way of reparation I said I'd mend his little Dinky car for him. A bit unfortunate because at one point the jack gave way and I was pinned to the carpet for three hours. In rushed my wife, she shouted to me 'Tiddles! Tiddles!' She's got a shocking memory for faces. In fact it's so bad on three occasions this week she's put lipstick and eye-shadow on the milkman. Or at least that's what he told the judge. 'Tiddles,' she said, 'I've just had two nasty accidents in the car. First I backed into a lamp-post, then I knocked down a keep-left sign, and then I ran right over Norman Tebbit's head.' I said 'Just a minute, that's three accidents.' She said 'No, only two *accidents*.' The trouble is she doesn't know her own strength. Yesterday she was throwing bread-crumbs to a starling and gave it concussion.

However, on to this joke, the one I haven't heard. I wonder what it can be about. Exciting isn't it? Isn't it? No, I do know it all takes place on board a ship. Which is rather interesting because last year we went on an exciting trip round the world. It was one of those special economy package deals. My wife and children went by sea, I went on a boat. Rather a thrill because it was the first time I'd been on a round-the-world cruise. When I say it was a round the world cruise, that was all a mistake. We were meant to be going to Guernsey, but we got out of Harwich and found there was no right turn. The captain was a very strange piece of work, he had a very rough wooden leg and a habit of sitting down and blistering his barnacles. But he did know how to throw a party. My goodness, food, drink, women, music . . . you hardly noticed they were missing. At the last party he threw I must admit things got a bit out of hand. I was sitting in the corner, still feeling a bit groggy after sampling the crow's nest soup, and it was quite obvious that the captain had had one or two. I blame the drink myself. And most of the crew were in a somewhat amphibious condition, singing songs like 'I'm in the mood for love' and 'It's impossible'. Then all at once a lady passenger leapt onto the table and proceeded to put away half a pint of lager, got half drunk, took off half her clothes, and half attempted to sing half a dirty rugby song. And ended up making a complete monocle of herself. Disgusting behaviour for a twenty-two-year-old woman. I was so shocked I almost dropped my Polaroid camera. Which by a strange coincidence has nothing whatever to do with the joke, which actually takes place aboard this American naval destroyer, where an urgent message has just come through on the radio to say that the father of one of the sailors, a sub-lieutenant Hiram J. Hennessy, has just passed away at his home in Seattle. And the rear-admiral calls in his captain and he says 'You're Hennessy's commanding officer, I think you should be the one to tell him.' So the captain radios through to Hennessy, who is down in the engine room, and as delicately as he can he breaks the tragic news. He says 'Hennessy, your old man's snuffed it. Over.' Well the rear-admiral, overhearing this, is disgusted. 'That is the most heartless thing I have ever witnessed,' he says. 'When you're telling someone a thing like

that you do it gently, soften the blow for the poor fellow.'
Well as luck would have it, a day later another message
comes through, this time for Petty Officer Schultzenheimer, to say that his mother has died. Actually she was
so upset by the death of Hiram J. Hennessy's father she
decided life wasn't worth living any more. And once again
it falls to the captain to break the news. So remembering
what he's been told he decides to try a different approach.
Instead of going straight to Schultzenheimer he puts out a
special order at 1800 hours for all the men to assemble on
deck. And when they're all there in front of him he calls for
silence and he says 'Right! All those with mothers take one
pace forward – Where d'you think *you're* going Schultzenheimer!!'

Pathetic, isn't it?

(*Ronnie is wearing a ludicrous cheap false nose on elastic.*)

Thank you. Now I know what you're thinking. 'What on earth is *that* stupid thing doing there? And why is it wearing a false nose?' Pathetic isn't it? A comedian of *my* calibre – small bore – having to resort to cheap visual gimmickry. Actually it was the producer's idea. Put it on, he said, you'll start the spot with a big laugh. I said 'I'm sorry, but our studio audience are intelligent, witty and sophisticated people . . . underneath . . . and they are far too mature just to laugh at a silly nose.'

(*He takes the false one off. The audience burst into laughter.*)

Oh I see! Thank you very much. Just for that I shall tell you a joke. Now this also comes from our producer, so if it doesn't seem all that funny we must make allowances, because at the time he told it he'd just been involved in a very nasty accident. He'd just bought a round of drinks. I don't think I'd be giving away trade secrets if I said he was very careful with his money, in fact they had to give him a general anaesthetic to take his wallet out. I think it all stems from his rather proper upbringing when he worked for five years as a Gentleman's Gentleman. A lavatory attendant. Until one day he got demoted and became a producer with BBC Light Entertainment. Anyway, he beckoned me over with his handbag, winked at me with his good eye, he said 'Ronald sweetie-pie.' I said 'Yes, Sugar-heart?' I'm not sure what he's got, but I'm convinced it's catching. He said 'Which old joke will you be finally laying to rest tonight then?' I said 'Well I've thought it over and I'm going to do the one about the chap who goes to the psychiatrist, because he's been feeling a bit mad, and the psychiatrist shows him one of these ink-blot tests. And he says "Now what do you think of when you look at this?" The chap examines it carefully and says "Sex". Whereupon the psychiatrist shows him another ink-blot. "And what do you think of when you look at this one," he says. Again the chap replies "Sex". Well, ten more ink-blots are shown to him and every time he gives the same answer: "Sex". Finally the psychiatrist slaps the book shut and says "My good man, it's my considered diagnosis that yours is an acute case of chronic rumpo-mania, in short that you are completely and utterly obsessed with sex." The chap says "*I'm* obsessed with sex! Who's been showing me all the dirty pictures?"'

Which, as a matter of fact, reminds me of the time *I* went to a psychiatrist a number of years ago, when everybody used to make comments about my size. In fact once when I was on holiday I went into a sportswear shop and asked for something I could lie on the sand in, they gave me an egg-timer.

Anyway, the producer unfortunately fell asleep before I'd finished the joke so I never found out whether he liked it. So instead I'm going to tell another one I happened to hear last week at the funeral of my old Uncle Cyrus, bless him. His death came as no great surprise to us. He was 94 years old and he'd just got married to a girl of eighteen, because he said he wanted to carry on the family strain. And of course it was too much for him. They were married on Saturday and we buried him the following Tuesday. We would have buried him on the Sunday but it took two days to wipe the smile off his face. But on with the joke, which is about a chap who is just about to go home from the pub one night, and not looking forward to it, and wondering to himself 'How hard will the wife hit my head with the rolling pin tonight? And will I have to take my cap off again with a bottle opener?' . . . when a man from a nearby group of revellers comes over and proposes a rather novel bet. He says 'You look like a sporting gent. I'll bet you a hundred pounds you can't do three things nominated by me and my friends here. I'll bet you can't drink ten pints of beer, wrestle a gorilla and make love to an Eskimo.' Well this being the sort of challenge you don't meet every day the chap takes the bet on there and then, and immediately consumes ten pints of the pub's best ale. The crowd are all obviously impressed, shouting 'Well done! . . . Bravo! . . . Pick him up!' And then they all go down to the local zoo where the chap gets into the cage with this grizzly-looking gorilla, and before you know it they're locked together, punches flying, fur all over the place, until finally the chap comes out, looking battered and bruised, but still clearly in one piece. And he dusts himself down proudly and says 'Right. Now let's go and wrestle the Eskimo.'

I'm told it's a letter

A bit of exciting news first of all – my great uncle
Hamish, who many of you will remember as the in-
ventor of the combined chastity-belt-cum-truss, for people
who need a little moral support, has just officially heard
that he's a father. He's been given twenty-eight days to
lodge an appeal. Oh, by the way, I nearly forgot. (*He takes
out a letter, excitedly.*) You see this? It came for me only this
morning. And I'm told, by people who know about these
things, that it's a letter. Now I know what you're thinking.
'Oh God, now he's had a letter we'll never hear the last of
it.' No, because this is nothing to me. I mean I get letters all
the time. I got another one once. And it can't have been all
that long ago because I can still remember it very clearly. It
had a black stamp on it. (*Opens the letter.*) No, this is
obviously just one of the hordes of letters I get constantly
from my many fanatically devoted followers and friends.
'Dear Squib-features.' You should see the letters I get from
my enemies. 'Dear Squib-features,' it says . . . Actually,
I've just realised who this letter is from, from the address at
the top here. 'Ward Six of the Ronnie Corbett Fan Club.'
No, it's from an old friend of mine, I remember now, who I
first met many years ago when we were both doing a rather
dismal summer season – Goering-on-Sea. I was appearing
in an act called The Three Kray Brothers. Actually it never
really hung together very well as an act. I used to come on in
a straw hat and sing three choruses of 'Mary from the Dairy'
while the other two sawed up a policeman. But this chap

was a great friend in those days, the sort of chap who would bend over backwards and go out of his way. A short-sighted limbo dancer. So it's interesting to see what he's got to say. 'Dear Squib-features. My wife and I can't begin to express our feelings of joy and unbounded excitement at your last show. Please can you tell us when it will be?' Who needs old friends?

Actually I seem to have wasted a bit of time there. Another black mark for me upstairs. The producer was getting very uptight with me earlier today, nervously fiddling with his rings. He wears these rings. Very cheap, very gaudy, and in my opinion far too big for his ears. He said to me 'I've been thinking.' A bit of a novelty. 'I've been thinking,' he said, 'there should be no more time-wasting in that chair of yours – just get on with it.' So here we go, with a story which all happened, as a matter of fact, when my wife and I were recently looking for a new house. Well our present one is in a bit of a state and undergoing some nasty subsidence. I first started getting suspicious when I came home one day up the garden path and tripped over the chimney. So there we are a week later, being shown round this brand new house by the estate agent. Not the most cheerful man; I don't know why he doesn't pack it in and go straight. We've known him a number of years. His wife was one of those women obsessed with beauty treatment and cosmetic operations. She had so much plastic surgery, when she died she left her body to Tupperware. Anyway, the chap's giving us all the sales talk. He said 'You'll notice, Mr Corbett, that this property has all the little extras that your present home lacks. Like . . . a roof, wall-to-wall floors, and an outside dustbin.' Suddenly, at this point, he stops talking, walks over to the window, and shouts out 'Green side up!' Then comes back over again. Well from there we went upstairs, looked round all the rooms, and in every one the same thing happened – he went over to the window and shouted out 'Green side up!' Well, after we'd seen the house from top to bottom I said 'Well, look, I'm bound to say I think the place is terrific. From my point of

view it's got everything. Plenty of room to stretch my legs
. . . a study . . . eye-level door-knobs,' I said, 'but there is
one slight thing that's nagging me. I can't help noticing that
wherever we go in the house, you keep leaning out the
window and shouting "Green side up!" ' He said 'Yes, I'm
afraid I have to do that – we've got a gang of Irishmen
outside, laying the lawn.'

All you need is a piece of chalk . . .

Y ou'll have to excuse me tonight if I seem a little bit
excited, but I can't keep it a secret any longer. Just
before I came on I received an urgent phone call from a lady
I used to go out with . . . my wife . . . saying I'd just landed
the title role in a fantastic new American TV series – *The
Bionic Dwarf.* I play what's left of the Six Million Dollar
Man after tax. It's all quite fascinating, he's like an automated version of James Bond, with lips powered by Ever
Ready and a nose that runs on batteries. I'm looking
forward to it all, dressing up as a mechanical man, although
I still have a few reservations about the dipstick, but there
we are. So I hope I can get through tonight's story, which I
can actually say is totally and absolutely brand new. I can
say that because I have no qualms at all about telling lies. In
fact I got this joke from Jimmy Tarbuck, who is something
of a connoisseur of good jokes. He leaves them to mature
for years in his cellar before he uses them. This particular
one is rather interesting, it's a 1953 Château Bernard
Manning. Full-bodied but with very little taste. By the way,
it's not been an easy week this week, what with the con-
tinued threat of BBC cutbacks and staff leaving all over the
place. Only the other day the BBC's Meteorological Department ground to a complete standstill, following the
shock resignation of the man who licks his finger and sticks
it out the window. He claimed he wasn't getting enough job

satisfaction. And now he's been offered a much more rewarding position at British Rail's public relations office, where he sticks two fingers out the window. They've even been cutting back on this show, I have to say. Instead of letting everybody get changed in private they've put us all into one room, with a big notice that says 'It's rude to point.'

Anyway here is the joke, which concerns a chap who is working late one night in the office with his gorgeous blonde secretary . . . I see the front row have just woken up. And as they're just finishing the paperwork the secretary leans across the desk and says 'Mr Masterson . . . (*sigh*) . . . It's getting very late Mr Masterson . . . (*sigh*) . . .' Because she got out of breath very easily this girl. A bit like my Uncle Sid, who has a lot of difficulty breathing these days. He's dead. No he isn't. That's just a story he puts around to gain sympathy. She says 'It's very late, Mr Masterson, don't you think it's time we were both in bed?' Well, being something of an opportunist this chap didn't need to stick *his* finger out the window to see which way the wind was blowing, so he ends up back at her place and a good time is had by all. Especially him. Well eventually he looks at his watch and says 'My God, my wife'll kill me!' So he quickly gets dressed and is about to rush off when the girl says 'Hang on, there's nothing to worry about. Just put this bit of chalk behind your ear, tell your wife exactly what happened, and you'll be fine.' So off he goes, gets home and there is his wife, sitting up in bed, sharpening the kitchen knife on her tongue, she says 'Where the hell have *you* been?' So, remembering what he's been told, the chap says 'Well, dear, I was working late with my beautiful secretary Fiona, and I'm afraid she invited me back to her flat and one thing led to another, and I ended up being unfaithful to you.' At which point the wife suddenly notices the piece of chalk sticking out behind his ear and says 'You ruddy liar, don't give me that – you've been down the pub again, playing darts!'

So much for democracy

Thank you and welcome to another edition of Ronnie Corbett Trots Out An Old Joke. Not the most scintillating of introductions is it? My original title for this spot was Ronnie Corbett Entertains – but they said that sounded more like a headline on *News at Ten*. And I'd probably be done under the Trades Descriptions Act. Which is the sort of publicity I can ill afford. Once again I am not exactly the flavour of the month here at the BBC. Thursday morning I got an official summons to the Director General's office – the D-G Leisure Centre as it's known here. He gets all the lavish treatment. He's got this sumptuous suite of offices on the first floor. It used to be on the second floor, then they moved it so he wouldn't have so far to reach for the lift button. To be honest I always get nervous going into swish offices because with my height if I stand on a thick carpet I get a nosebleed. And I did rather blot my copybook on this occasion. I somewhat thoughtlessly barged straight in, only to find he was having lunch with the Prime Minister. There she was tucking into her bowl of tripe . . . I said 'I knew you'd eat your words sooner or later.' Now I don't know why I said that. To get a cheap laugh I suppose. Not unnaturally it got things off to a shaky start. After she'd left, the D-G beckoned me back in; he said 'Sit yourself down, Cornett. Anywhere on the floor will be fine.' Then he sat there puffing away at his cigar for several minutes . . . until he finally got the wrapper off. I think he's a bit out of condition myself. He leant back in his power-assisted

61

swivel-chair and said 'The fact of the matter is Cornett, it's these quips you keep coming out with. I've been getting complaints. Now either you buck your ideas up or you'll go straight back where you came from – as a stunt man for the Tetley Tea Folk.' So to make sure I'm in the clear this week I've decided to let the audience choose the joke. Any subject you like, and I will tell a joke about it. Just shout it out.

(*The audience shout in unison: 'Two brothers who inherit two horses!'*)

What was that? Two brothers who inherit two horses did somebody say? So much for democracy. Now if the Director General is watching I know what he's thinking: he told them to say that before he came on, the devious little liar. Because he's like that, I'm afraid. A very good judge of character. So these two brothers inherit these two horses . . . I think we've just about set up the plot now haven't we? They inherit two horses, and . . . that's six bloody horses they've inherited now. And one of them says 'Duhhh . . . we've got two horses, uhhhh . . .' He wasn't all that bright, this particular brother. 'Uhhhh . . . we got two horses, I say we split them down the middle.' Metaphorically speaking, that is, because they were not in the hamburger game. And the other brother says 'Yeah . . . duhhhh . . . we'll divide them equally between us.' He was a damned sight thicker than his brother. 'We'll divide them equally,' he said, 'which means that you'll have one . . . and . . . uhh . . . I'll have . . . the other one.' Sounds like a meeting at the Treasury, doesn't it? So having taken a horse each they are faced with the problem of how to recognise which is which, and one of them has a bright idea, he says 'I know . . . uhhh . . . I'll dock my horse's tail. Then we'll know which is yours and which is mine.' So they do this, but the following morning they find some practical joker has gone and docked the other horse's tail as well, so now both horses have got docked tails. Then they have another idea. Two in one week, it was a record. One of the brothers nicks a little bit out of his horse's ear. 'Brilliant,' says his brother. 'Now we'll definitely know which is which.' Of course, the next morning, the prankster has been at work again, and nicked the other horse's ear as well. So the two brothers have a think about the problem, and then one of them solves it. 'I know,' he says. 'I've got it. You have the black one, I'll have the white one.'

Here is a very cheap joke

Here is a very funny joke which I picked up cheap the other Friday at our local jumble sale. And . . . oh, incidentally, at various points during this story a man over there will hold up a big card with 'LAUGH' on it. Take no notice of him. He's got laryngitis. Come to think of it, it was Thursday I went to the jumble sale, because Friday was the thirteenth and I never go out on Friday the thirteenth, because I happen to be very superstitious. Ever since the disaster that occurred the last time I walked under a ladder. I clean forgot the budgie was still up it. My wife warned me – 'On your own head be it,' she said, and she was right. *She* can talk! I suppose that's obvious otherwise how could she say 'On your own head be it'? But she can be pretty careless herself at times. When she buys those big packets of sandpaper sheets for the budgie cage I'll swear she doesn't study the instructions. All right if you like smooth budgies. Ours is getting thinner every time I see it. Anyway she said to me 'Why don't you take the kids down to the vicar's jumble sale? You never know, they might fetch a few quid.' Now actually I'm doing it again – wandering off the point. Which could be fatal tonight because I've already had two public warnings from the high echelons of the BBC. This lunchtime I was in the canteen, carbon-dating a piece of burnt toast, and . . . that's an exaggeration, but the service up there is incredibly slow. Would you believe the meals take so long now they have to put mothballs in the jacket potatoes? It may sound revolting but it does improve the flavour.

But I digress, and on with this joke I got at the jumble sale. This chap goes to see his doctor. 'Doctor,' he says, 'I feel a bit rough. Or so my wife tells me. And I'm rather worried I'm losing a lot of weight.' Well the doctor has him undress, which is rather a disturbing sight because he is incredibly thin, this chap, with a very hairy chest. With his shirt off he looked like a toothbrush. And the doctor examines him thoroughly with his telescope – I forgot to tell you he was very shy – and he says 'In my opinion you've been overworking. What you need is a complete break. Get away from crowds altogether. Go and see Ronnie Corbett in cabaret.' Little plug for my cabaret act there, which to be honest is going through a bad patch. These days I do an hour and a half, then the audience elect a foreman and go away to consider their verdict. Sometimes if it's going really well I invite one or two members of the audience up and do a card trick. Sometimes I invite them all up and we have a game of bridge. Anyway, this chap goes home to his wife. Actually I must point out this is not the happiest of marriages, because the fact is they're total opposites. He's a man, she's a woman. He's thin, she has to use a funnel to get into bed. So he goes home and there is his wife in the front room, ironing the cat. She's very house-proud. She's the sort of woman who puts a hairnet on a peach. And he tells her what the doctor has said, he says 'There's only one thing for it, a holiday.' 'About time too,' says his wife. 'I haven't had a decent holiday in years.' 'How can you say that?' he ripostes. 'What about that place we went last year – loads of sand, temperatures in the nineties, the dark-skinned natives toiling at their local crafts . . .' She said 'I'm sorry, Brixton Cement Works isn't my idea of whoopee.' He said 'Well never mind, I've been making enquiries and I've fixed up to spend a fantastic summer this year in Morocco.' She said 'That sounds fantastic, I can't wait to see what it looks like.' He said 'You won't have to wait long, I'll send you a postcard.' She said 'You miserly

66

old skinflint, you don't mean you're going there without me?' He said 'Well look, dearest treasure of my heart, this holiday wouldn't suit you at all. Because I have found a somewhat naughty Arab quarter, where apparently the husbands have so many girls in their harems they actually pay gentlemen seven pounds a time to provide a night of passion for one of their wives.' His wife said 'Right, in that case I'm definitely coming with you.' He said 'Why?' She said 'I can't wait to see how you get by on fourteen quid a month.'

For Their Eyes Only

It was very interesting watching the serial earlier on wasn't it? Man's struggle against the Iron Fist of a monstrous tyranny, battling against a regime of relentless, soul-crushing repression. It's just like working at the BBC. And for anyone who doubts it, I have managed to obtain here one of the BBC's top secret personal files. On Yours Truly. Frightening isn't it? How many MPs, I wonder, would sleep soundly in their secretaries' beds if they knew that the BBC keeps a highly personal file on every one of its employees – from the lowliest tea boy, right down to the producer of this show. All the files are locked away in the bowels of Television Centre, just next to the place where they keep the studio audiences. *They* have to be locked up for their own good. Thirteen audiences the BBC have got now. They did have fourteen, but last week one of them died. Well they didn't just die, you know. They were watching a recording of *Wogan* and they lost the will to live. Don't tell me, you know how they feel. Now this document is of course highly confidential and top-secret and only the Chairman of the BBC himself must ever be allowed to read what's in this file. (*He opens it and reads.*) 'Name. Ronald Goliath Corbett.' My parents were nothing if not optimists. 'Ronald Goliath Corbett. Staff number 23704 and a half. Sex. Satisfactory progress.' Oh no, I'm reading the wrong bit there, sorry. No I'm not. How dare they? 'Occupation. Sits in a chair and tells long, rambling stories. Nobody knows why. Physical peculiarities . . .' (*He reads silently for several seconds, turning over the page.*) They've missed one out, surely. Oh no, there it is. I must remember to block up the key-hole to my dressing room in future. 'General comments. This man was funny once. The occasion was the 4th June 1972, when an audience laughed at one of his stories. He was later fined for failing to report an accident. These days constantly resorts to cheap jokes about deprived childhood to gain audience sympathy.' Well that is patently untrue, I actually had a very happy childhood. Sunday afternoons, playing piggy in the middle with a ham sandwich . . . I won't pretend my parents were well off, in fact I was the only baby down our road with a self-assembly rusk. Because my father did have seventeen children and was very short of cash. He was pretty short of breath too, as a matter of fact. And as a little toddler I always had to sleep in the same bed with my sixteen sisters. We used to lie there and play snap, and I always lost. So it's just not true to say I keep doing jokes about my childhood. Anyway where were we? 'Director General's comments, if printable. Nothing is more enjoyable to me than watching Ronnie Corbett telling a joke on a Saturday night. So in future I am going to watch nothing. I particularly dislike him because he is such an inquisitive little nosey parker . . .' That's a downright lie! I am not nosey at all . . . 'In that case, why are you reading this confidential top-secret document?' (*Slams it shut.*)

I think that's quite enough of that. On to tonight's story which is something of a desperate choice. It pains me to admit I actually got this joke out of Bernard Manning's dustbin. Rather a risky thing to do, because he was still wearing it. And it all concerns this little boy who has an absolute mania for eating toffee. All day long all he eats is toffee. Sticks of toffee, slabs of toffee, nothing but toffee. And his mother is at her wit's end. Fortunately she's just managed to wean her other son off lollipops by telling him they make your hair fall out. An idea she got while watching Kojak. So she tells the little boy that eating toffee makes you fat. She says 'If you go on eating all this toffee you'll grow big and gross and overweight and no one will love you any more.' You can see why Bernard Manning threw this away can't you. So the weeks go by and all the time the boy's mother is drumming it into him. 'Eating toffee makes you big and fat.' Well a month or so later they're both sitting on the bus and directly opposite them is a young lady of a rather pregnant nature. So the little boy notices this and naturally keeps looking at her. Incidentally, it would be very easy at this stage to mix this story up with the other one, you know, about the young school-mistress who keeps staring at a vicar at the other end of the bus. And then he passes her to get off and she says 'I'm dreadfully sorry, I thought you were the father of one of my children.' It's very lucky it's not that one. So the little boy now can't take his eyes off the expectant young mother-to-be, and he starts winking at her. Eventually the lady gets rather distressed, she says 'I beg your pardon, sonny, but do you know me?' And the boy says 'No, but I know what you've been doing!'

First some bad language

Thank you. *Dank je wel.* Now tonight . . . by the way how many of you noticed? Just then, I slipped in a bit of German. I didn't do that just to impress you, it was actually for the benefit of our new German au pair. She's a bit homesick so I'll say a few words in her native tongue to cheer her up . . . *Heil Hitler!* No she's very sweet, she said to me 'I hope you will be forgiving me my extremely bad language. But my grandma still needs much touching up.' You can laugh, you haven't seen her grandma. However, on to tonight's story, which was actually handed down to me by my dear old grandfather – last night as he was clearing out the attic. I suppose I should have gone up there myself but with my height climbing a ladder can be quite an ordeal. Like the last time when I pitched camp for the night on the fourth rung and ran out of supplies. Besides which my grandfather, in spite of his age, is remarkably fit. Ninety-two and still doing all the things he was doing when he was twenty-two. The other night I peeped in his bedroom door and saw two sets of false teeth in his glass. The next day he was walking round with another notch on his walking stick.

Anyway, this joke was found in an old scrapbook, that actually contained all the rave reviews of my past performances. I let go at one point and it nearly floated out the window. Looking through it brought back a lot of memories because I had some very strange jobs back in the old days. For two years I went round the music halls as the back half of Jessie Matthews. I'll never forget one theatre where they'd accidentally double-booked fourteen strip-tease dancers and a flea circus. At the last moment everything had to be scratched. Then I joined a travelling sideshow with the Fattest Man in the World. It was very tragic, his stomach came right out here, and in the end he died of curiosity. But I must get on with this joke because to be honest I'm still feeling a bit groggy tonight, I've just had a tooth out. It started aching on Tuesday night as I was watching that late-night film about Ivan the Terrible, and his wife Blodwyn the Extremely Disappointed. And it was plaguing me at rehearsals, so I went along to the BBC Emergency Dental Service. No appointment necessary, you just go up to a gang of scene shifters and tell them to get a bloody move on.

So on with the joke. Which concerns these two rugby players, who are both spending their summer holidays at Scarborough for a bet. One day for a thrill they go to the local fairground. And one of them says 'Rodney darling . . .' Actually when I say they were rugby players that isn't strictly true. I just put that in to win back some of the Welsh viewers, who switched off after the line about Ivan the Terrible. And I failed. The chap says 'Rodney darling, why don't we have a go on the ferris wheel.' His friend says 'You can go on, Terry, but it looks far too dangerous for me. I'll stay here and watch.' So off goes the first chap on his own, onto this huge fairground wheel, and as it goes faster and faster he suddenly loses his grip and is thrown right off the wheel into the air, and lands on the ground below. And straightaway everyone rushes round him, and his friend, who's been watching all this in horror, pushes his way through the crowd and comes across this prostrate body; he says 'Terry! Terry! Are you hurt?' The other chap lifts himself onto one elbow, he says 'I should say I'm hurt, I went round three times and you never waved once!'

I could have been the new Charles Bronson

Tonight I'd like to tell you a very, very funny joke. This is the sort of joke that will still be loved and enjoyed even when it's a hundred years old. A week next Tuesday. Why do I bother? Why do I carry on every week when you consider that for three times the money I could go and work for British Rail? Who says crime doesn't pay? If I'd gone into films, by now I could have matured into a huge, international sex symbol. You can laugh. Did they explain that to you when you came in? No, but for a strange quirk of fate I could have been the new Charles Bronson. If the old one had been a pint-sized comedian who wore glasses. Actually I'm being unfair to myself there – all these stories I keep putting around about being small. Like when I say that for three months I served as a shop steward on a silicon chip. That's all just part of my professional repertoire. The truth is I've always been a bit sensitive about my physique, since that time I went into hospital. I took off all my clothes, and the doctor rushed over and gave me the kiss of life. I suppose really I should never have got undressed in the first place – strictly speaking my wife wasn't even allowed visitors. As it happens I was admitted myself, shortly afterwards. I'd been feeling very weak and tired and nothing the doctors did seemed to help. In the end they put me on a course of iron tablets and I collapsed with metal fatigue. You see people never take me seriously. Like the dressing rooms they give me here at the BBC. You won't believe this but until a month ago I was still classified as a glove puppet. Until the start of each show I was kept folded up in a biscuit tin with Roland Rat. Worst of all must be this set – a box with a chair on it. Well this week my pride got the better of me and I complained to the Managing Director of Television. He said 'Don't worry about a thing. As from this week I'm giving the whole set a facelift. More sparkle, more glitter, more razzamatazz,' he said. 'You won't even recognise it.'

(*We reveal a solitary pink balloon tied to the back of the chair.*)

Isn't it pathetic? Little things please little minds, I suppose. (*He takes out a long knitting needle.*) Shall I? If only it were that simple. Do you realise that one stab with this and I could cause a national walk-out by the National Federation of Balloon-popping Operatives? Which could seriously disrupt Faith Brown's acupuncture course. So I won't bother. Why should I descend to their level? Minds like children all of them. Oh that reminds me, a little wave to my own children. Only things have been a bit iffy at home again lately. The riots in the hamster's cage are just entering their fifth week, and on Monday afternoon our little boy became very distraught when his piggy bank contracted swine fever. Added to which last weekend our young puppy dog was sniffing round the front room and accidentally swallowed the remote control gadget for the TV. A bit unfortunate – now we have to twiddle his tummy to get BBC 1. If we want ITV we have to twiddle the top of his left leg. Thank God we never watch BBC 2.

Anyway, on to the joke, which concerns this rather posh, well-to-do lady from Belgravia, who one day takes her young son for a day out to the local cattle show. And the son is all agog because he's never seen a cow close up before. Well he's seen bits of them, you know, nestling by the Yorkshire pudding. But he's never seen what they look like all put together. And as they're standing there looking at one particular cow, an old farmer comes up and starts feeling the animal all along its flank, pressing the skin and kneading its muscles . . . I think he was trying to get BBC 2, actually. And the boy turns to his mummy and says 'Mummy.' Because he knows her quiet well. 'Mummy,' he says, 'what's the man doing that for?' His mother says 'Well he's got to do that, that tells him how much meat there is on the cow and if he thinks there's enough he'll buy it, you see.' It's quite educational this joke isn't it? That's about all it is. So a couple of days later the boy is sitting at the breakfast table in the family's plush mansion, tucking into his quadrophonic rice crispies, and wearing a bit of a frown, so his mother asks him what's on his mind. He says 'Well, you know what you told me the other day about that farmer and the cow at the cattle market?' She says 'Yes?' He says 'Well I was just walking past the kitchen a few minutes ago, and I think Daddy wants to buy the cook.'

The Black Death wasn't funny either

Thank you very much. Woof woof. Now tonight . . . By the way, how many of you noticed that I went woof woof just then? I'll tell you why I did that, because this weekend I received a rather charming letter from a cocker spaniel. Well obviously that's not strictly true, I didn't actually receive a letter from a cocker spaniel. It was a whippet. I just said it was a cocker spaniel to try and make it more interesting. The first dog I ever owned myself was a cocker spaniel, only he had to go after he disgraced himself. He wandered into the bedroom one day and thought I was a bone. I spent the weekend tunnelling out of the back garden. I was ready for him the next time, though. He went for me in the bathroom and bit off more than he could chew. However, this whippet that wrote to me is the honorary secretary of the new Dog Language Society, the ones who are campaigning for a new TV station on which everybody barks. You've probably seen them on the news, they go round digging up signposts . . . well not exactly *digging* up signposts, but doing something up signposts. Anyway, he asked if I'd kindly say a few words in Dog language for all the dogs who are looking in tonight. So there we are. Woof Woof. Woof woof woof woof. Amazingly lifelike isn't it. Yet another talent. As a matter of fact I learnt how to speak fluent Dog while still at college, where I studied under a chihuahua.

But quickly on to tonight's joke. Now any blame for this joke I'm going to tell tonight must rest squarely on the shoulders of my agent, Shamus El Bloomstein. A man of somewhat mixed parentage. He's actually part Moslem, part Hebrew and part Catholic. Three times a day he kneels towards Mecca and sings Oi Vay Maria. Now I know my agent very well, he's like one of the family. Like my Aunty Ethel. As a matter of fact we both grew up together in this very rough neighbourhood. Well *he* grew up, I sort of never really bothered. And it was a very violent area, people were afraid to go *anywhere*. One chap got mugged turning over in bed. It was the only town in the district where the local paper had a Forthcoming Deaths column. And there were some real sharks operating in the high street. Well not *real* sharks. That would be a bit ridiculous. In the middle of Arbroath on a Thursday. But my agent was at that time running a rather shady undertaker's business. Fifty pounds for a new pine coffin, with a ten-quid trade-in on your old one. Anyway, I happened to run into him last week while I was out shopping. I'd just popped into our local chemist's to get measured up for an Elastoplast. As a matter of fact the service in our chemist's is now so slow they've opened a little off-licence bar for you to wait in. It's quite nice, you can get a pint of draft Optrex, or penicillin in a basket, or a packet of smoky Valium crisps. Or if you prefer it they do a running buffet of Andrews Liver Salts. However before I left him he did remind me of this joke, which was actually the first joke I ever told as a comedian. Rather appropriate, because tonight is in fact the anniversary of my entry into show business. As of tonight my career as a comic has lasted exactly twenty-five years. Or as one critic pointed out, two years longer than the Black Death.

Anyway, here is the joke, which is about a golfer who one day turns up at his clubhouse brandishing this new golf ball. 'You are here looking,' he says, 'at the most ingenious golf ball ever produced. It is absolutely impossible to lose. If you hit it into some long grass it will automatically emit a very loud, high-pitched bleeping noise. If you hit it into a river or a lake it will immediately rise to the surface and start flashing bright orange. And if by any accident you should slice it into a clump of bushes or a tree, a miniaturised tape recorder inside it will blare out 'I'm over here you fool!' Well on hearing this, the assembled company at the bar are dumbstruck. 'Well I never,' they say . . . and 'Bless my soul!' . . . and 'Don't cry for me Argentina.' And one of them gets up and says 'That is truly the most incredible golf ball I have ever come across in all my puff. Where on earth did you get it?' And the chap says 'I found it.'

Tarzan, Lord of the Field-mice

Here is a story about a man who, for thirty-five years, has been a supporter of Fulham Football Club. Pathetic isn't it. Another story of low life. Actually I know what you're thinking. Here we go, just an excuse to do a lot of cheap jokes about Fulham. Well you're wrong. Because I happen to be Fulham Football Club's biggest fan. Which will give you some idea how many fans they've got. As a matter of fact I suddenly remembered this joke at lunchtime in the BBC Club. Our director was lying underneath a table, carrying out auditions, and my agent, who had just been making a phone call, came back to the table, checked the dipstick in his Perrier Water . . . he's not exactly a heavy drinker. He once took three weeks to dry out after eating a wine gum. However he had some exciting news – I have just been picked for the title role in the next Tarzan movie. Called *Tarzan Isn't Very Well*. Next week I begin rehearsing my first big scene with Bo Derek. She'll be in a very revealing low-cut loincloth and I'll be in a fall-out shelter. To be honest I'm hoping it will buck me up a bit because I've been very tense this week. I saw the doctor about it and he got out one of those things that tests your blood pressure. A rates demand. Then he had me take off all my clothes, examined me from top to bottom, and said 'I can find nothing at all wrong with you, Mrs Corbett.' Personally I don't think he's got much idea. I asked him for something to slow me down once and he gave me a pint of brake fluid. I know why I was feeling tense, it's this new house I was telling you about. There are still a lot of teething troubles. On Monday we had a setback when we heard the cockroaches in the bedroom had been given six months security of tenure.

But I digress. And back to this joke I remembered. As a matter of fact I remembered two jokes. The other one was that story about the very rich oil tycoon who is deciding what to buy his three sons for Christmas. And the first son says he'd like a boat, so he buys him the QE2. The second son says he'd like a music centre so he buys him the Albert Hall. And the youngest son says he'd like a cowboy outfit, so he buys him British Airways. Unfortunately I haven't got time to tell that joke, besides which I prefer the sporting flavour of the other one, as I am myself something of a sports enthusiast. That sounds hard to believe when you consider that at school I was a bit of weakling. Let's face it, at our school everybody was a weakling. We were the only side who had to bring on a substitute for ring-a-ring-a-roses. And I've never forgotten the day my brother and I took part in the three-legged race. We tied the wrong legs together and spent two hours running round in circles. And all the risky things we used to get up to, like playing conkers in the showers. That really kept you on your toes.

However, to return to the chap, remember? Who supports Fulham FC. One day he goes along to the club secretary and he says 'I've supported your club religiously all my life. When I die, as a gesture of my loyalty to the club, I'd like my ashes to be scattered over the ground.' So the secretary says 'Well I don't know about that, spectators aren't really allowed on the pitch. I've got a better idea, why don't you go and see a taxidermist?' Sounds a bit like my bank manager. 'See a taxidermist,' he says, 'and arrange something with him, and then what we'll do is sit you back in your old place in the stand every Saturday afternoon.' So the chap agrees to this, and the years go by and eventually the fateful day comes round. He's sitting at home listening to Derek Jameson on the radio and he dies in his sleep. Well, all the instructions he left were carried out to the letter, and the following Saturday, at three o'clock they sat him in his old place in the stand at Fulham Football Ground. And as usual he left at half time.

'Thousands have laughed at my Malvolio . . .'

Tonight we're all a bit excited because one of the camera crew has just got into the Guinness Book of Records. Earlier this evening he set up a new world record for the longest a BBC cameraman has gone without a drink. Twenty-seven yards. To be honest, I'm feeling a bit drained tonight, because I spent the weekend pot-holing – actually I was in the back garden, trying to pull up a worm and it got the better of me. I was out there trying to do a spot of gardening. A bit of a thankless task. Once again our annual vegetable crop has been a disaster. We must be the only family in Surrey who peel the carrots with a pencil-sharpener. As usual the cabbage patch is a waste land. In fact the caterpillars have grown incredibly fat. My wife found one at the bottom of the garden and thought it was an unexploded bomb. Of course if she wasn't so fussy the garden wouldn't be in the state it is. Would you believe we took six months to lay a lawn because she couldn't decide on the colour? As a matter of fact things have never been right with that lawn, because she got the grass seed mixed up with the bird seed, and twice a week we have to mow the budgie. The trouble is she doesn't really think about what she's doing. I'll never forget last bonfire night. A bit of a memorable evening in itself, because that was the occasion I got my shoelace caught on a rocket and spent the night on the church roof. Well my wife had found out that when you light a Catherine wheel you can make it go round, so she went indoors and set fire to the housekeeping money. I shouldn't really moan because in these hard times it pays to be careful. Every January, even now, we still go and fight our way through the sales at our local DIY store – the Texas Chain-store Massacre as it's become known. I learnt the value of money during my rather Spartan childhood. I always remember the first proper Christmas dinner we ever had, my mother served up a kipper with two Brussels sprouts on top. I never forgave her for that, I thought she'd killed a mermaid. In fact my mother had a rather interesting job, helping to preserve stained glass. She was a window-cleaner for British Rail.

But I digress. There is a small theatrical touring company who arrive mid-week in this rather bleak, pokey dead-and-alive town . . . nowhere near Watford. No, I must make that clear from the outset, because I wouldn't want a lot of angry calls from people in Watford. Well it's possible. Some of them are on the phone there now. I mean it's an incredible responsibility really, when you think that I'm sitting here being watched by twelve, thirteen, maybe even fourteen people. I do have to be very careful. So this theatrical company arrive in town, and the leading light of the group, a rather grand actor-manager type, strolls into the local butcher's shop with his silver-topped cane and says 'Good day to you, Butcher. My name is Sir Balthazar Pules, world famous thespian. Thousands have laughed at my Malvolio. And I was wondering if you'd be kind enough to cash me a small cheque?' Whereupon he unfolds this cheque and holds it up to the butcher, who squints at it closely and then says, politely but firmly: 'Naff off, ponce-features.' Whereupon the chap carefully folds the cheque up, puts it back in his pocket and leaves. Then he goes next door to the baker's – same thing again. 'My name is Sir Balthazar Pules, would you be kind enough to cash me a small cheque?' Once again the same reply: 'On your bike.' So once again he folds the cheque up, puts it back in his pocket and leaves. This happens in every shop in the street.

He goes to the grocer's, the fishmonger's, the tailor's, the ironmonger's, even to the man on the corner selling matches, who unfortunately only takes Diner's Club. And everywhere it's the same story. Finally he arrives at the laundry. He goes in, takes the cheque out of his pocket and unfolds it. 'My name is Sir Balthazar Pules.' And the chap behind the counter says 'I'm sorry, we don't cash cheques.' He says 'I don't want you to cash it, I want you to iron it.'

What to do if you hunger after sex

I'd like if I may, tonight, to relate a joke exactly as it was told to me by our producer. Well not exactly as it was told to me by the producer, obviously. That would look a bit ridiculous, hanging from a chandelier with an ice bucket over my head. Although I have to say that since he told me this story our producer has stopped *that* . . . (*shakes hand*) . . . drying his nail varnish. He has also stopped drinking, in fact these days he's abstemious to a fault. He even takes soda with a Scotch egg. Well we all have to be careful. As a matter of fact I've been on a bit of a health kick recently. I've been trying my hand at yoga without too much success. Last weekend I was practising on the floor of the sitting room and got both my big toes stuck in my ears. For an hour and a half my children took it in turns to knock me over and watch me bounce back up again. I've also been trying a bit of heat therapy, and bought one of those sun ray lamps. It was actually recommended to me by a BBC weather forecaster. You leave it on for six minutes and it turns into a shower. Which reminds me of an incident I wanted to tell you about, because the other afternoon I was lying in the bath, playing I-spy with the window cleaner . . . my five-year-old son was outside redecorating the front door, which I'd told him was a painting by numbers kit . . . and my wife was in one of her sulks. We had a bit of a row the other morning. The postman had just delivered my weekly stack

91

of fan mail – one letter. On the front of the envelope it said 'To the funniest man on television' and my wife had sent it back marked 'Not known at this address'. Anyway, as I was saying, I was in the bath, when all of a sudden the phone rang. It was the producer on the line. He said 'Is that you, dear?' He calls me dear – he obviously hasn't read my contract. He was actually ringing up to see if I wanted to go on this year's BBC staff outing. Every year the BBC organise one of these mystery tours. For £6.50 you get a skateboard and a blindfold. This year they were trying something a little bit different, an off-peak trip to Cleethorpes. So I rather foolishly said I'd go, and of course it was a total disaster. The Head of Comedy, who is a bit on the snooty side – the sort of man who eats candy floss with a knife and fork – refused to go into the hall of mirrors, because he never sees himself without an appointment. And I can tell you things weren't any livelier when we went on the beach. The Punch and Judy puppets were both away at an Equity branch meeting, and at one point a seagull flew overhead and was reported as a UFO.

Anyway, I digress. Visualise, if you can, this old Scottish priest up in the Highlands, who is one day delivering a sermon to his assembled flock on the subject 'What to do if you hunger after sex. Keep a packet of biscuits on the bedside table.' No, he didn't say that. He was actually a very eloquent and fiery speaker, and his sermon was such a hit that after he's done three encores and was standing outside, autographing hymn-sheets, his young curate comes up to him and says 'That was the most brilliant thing I have ever heard. How I wish I had the confidence to deliver a sermon like that.' So the priest takes the curate back into the church and from a little ledge just behind the pulpit he takes out a small bottle and he says 'Afore ye get up to speak son, just take a wee snort of this gin, and it'll give ye all the confidence ye need.' So the following Sunday the curate delivers his sermon, and afterwards goes to the priest to ask how it went. And the priest says 'Well it was very vivid, son, and very moving, but there are just one or two points I'd like to make. First of all, when you've finished I'd rather you didn't tear your notes up and throw them over the congregation. When you leave the pulpit it's better to walk down the steps and not slide down the banister. And the correct phrase is "David *slew* Goliath". He didn't knock seven bells out of him. Finally, and most important,' he said, 'David's sling was full of shot.'

Thank you for all your letters

This is a rather amusing story which I used to tell in my early days as a comedian. It's funny actually, but I can still remember the very first time I got a laugh. I wish I could remember the last time. Incidentally thank you for all your letters. No, I say that from the heart because I have always been very unlucky when it comes to mail. I once received a stripper-gram which was opened in error by the bloke next door. And the only proper letter I've had this year was a final demand from BUPA. And if you don't pay up they come round and dislocate your elbow. Talking of mail, incidentally, there was a very interesting item on the news about a team of archaeologists, who have just discovered the entrance to an ancient Egyptian tomb which has not been opened for 3,000 years. And they had to use a mechanical digger to get through the *Reader's Digest* circulars. By the way I hope my wife is watching tonight because she was in a bit of a snit earlier on. I don't know why she was upset, all I did was put in a gumshield to eat one of her fairy cakes, and she burst into tears. A bit of a mood developed thereafter – time was going so slowly, at one point the cuckoo threw itself out of the clock. Then I got this phone call from an old friend who used to be a war-time comedian and is now a big theatrical impresario. My goodness, he's come a long way since he used to do the warm-up for the Nuremberg Rallies. And he was all excited about this big new show he was putting on. He said 'This'll be the smash-hit musical of all time, Ron. Guess what – we've got

Streisand playing the lead!' I said 'That's terrific – Barbra Streisand!' He said 'No, Mabel Streisand. She's not very well known yet, but given time I think she could be really big. And in any case, with music by Rice and Lloyd-Webber we'll be on to a sure-fire winner.' I said 'Well that's marvellous, Tim Rice and Andrew Lloyd-Webber are the tops.' He said 'No, this is Bert Rice and Percy Lloyd-Webber. Nobody in this country's heard of them yet, but just you wait. And listen to this,' he said. 'The star comedian is a chap named Boyce.' I said 'Not Max Boyce?' He said 'Yes, that's him.' Well, my wife and I went along to the premiere because we don't tend to get out a lot these days. The last time I took her out was to the local civic hall to see Big Daddy and Giant Haystacks. That was the night they split their tights and gave a display of all-out wrestling. I had offered to take my wife to the 1981 Labour Party Conference, but she can't stand blood sports so we didn't bother. So there we are at this glittering gala, rubbing shoulders with beautiful actresses . . . well in my case not rubbing shoulders, but having a good time generally.

And it was there that I was reminded of this joke, which takes place at the end of the last century in one of the last remote outposts of the British Empire. Ealing Broadway. Not it's not Ealing Broadway. Picture, if you will, a small garrison of British soldiers in the baking hot South African province of Natal, where one day a new army chaplain arrives, and straightaway he goes along to see the colonel who's in charge. He says 'Good morning I'm your new chaplain.' I should explain he's a bit wet this man, his dog collar has a little bell on it. He says 'My name is the Wight Wevewend Wodney Wenfwew-Woberts. Fwom Wothewam.' The colonel says 'Welcome to the regiment, I'm sure you'll have a cracking time here. We have a smashing social life. Every Wednesday all the lads get together in the mess, drink till they're sick as a pig, and then fall over. You'll love it.' The chap says 'Well actually I'm afwaid I don't actually appwove of dwinking.' The colonel says 'Oh well, you'll like Thursdays. That's the night we have a bunch of the local native girls over. You'll love that. Ravishing women. All night long if you're lucky.' The chap says 'Look I'm tewwibly sowwy, but I don't much go in for that sort of thing with ladies.' The colonel says 'My God! You don't mean to say you're . . . I mean, you're not telling me you're a . . . that you're actually a bit of a . . .' The chap says 'Why certainly not!' He says 'Oh, well in that case you won't enjoy Friday nights either.'

Ear-syringing was on special offer

This week I'd like to remind you of the joke about the woman whose husband dies, and her friend calls round and says 'I was so sorry to hear about your tragic loss. What did he die of, was it food poisoning?' The woman said 'No.' She said 'Was it pneumonia?' She said 'No.' She said 'Was it a heart attack?' She said 'No.' So she said, 'Oh – nothing serious then.' Now the reason I mention that story is because I recently had the misfortune to go down with something a bit nasty myself. I was just preparing to do a bit of work on our window box, and was pulling my wellington boots on in readiness, when I suddenly became doubled up with pain, so I went straight round to our local GP. Now there's a man with a head for business. At his practice, with all orders for barbiturates over four bottles you get a free hernia check and a blood transfusion. And Tuesdays and Fridays he gives quadruple stamps with every prescription for the Pill. My wife and I have worked it out, in ten years time we'll have enough for a set of teaspoons. Of course all this commercialism can be very embarrassing. I know one chap who went to see him about a rather personal sexual hang-up, and he came away with a free set of tights. Anyway, when I arrived there it was a bit crowded, because ear-syringing was on special offer, and there was a big notice up in the waiting room 'All vasectomies must go!' So he gave me an examination and said I should go along to the hospital, which was not exactly guaranteed to restore my confidence. Believe me, life is no bed of roses at St Methuselah's General. The only hospital in Britain with horse-drawn ambulances. Added to which they're not even very good drawings. As I got there there was a bit of a panic on because one of the leeches had escaped, and the senior registrar, who was ninety-two if he was a day, was attempting to chase it across the floor. Now unfortunately the hospital's top specialist in abdominal disorders wasn't actually there; he'd been held up at a rain-making ceremony in Malawi. And so not to put too fine a point on it, I was getting a bit nervous. Especially when one of the nurses tied a little tag round my wrist and said 'This is just so the surgeon doesn't make any mistakes.' At which point I looked at the tag, and it said 'Hand'. Then the nurse came back and said 'Here comes your surgeon now, you can put your trust in this man completely.' I said 'That's all very well, but why is he wearing a black armband?' And I think I would have been more frightened still if I'd known then what I know now – that he was actually a failed pork butcher, and apparently notorious for dropping a patient's appendix into the bowl and saying 'Just under half a pound, is that all right madam?'

So how I survived I don't know, but I've just about recovered enough to tell you this joke, about a cowboy who is sitting in the saloon bar, when suddenly a man comes in and says 'Say, pardnur, is that your horse a-standin' out there, yonder?' Because he hadn't take any acting lessons, this man. The cowboy said 'Why shucks and goodness gracious me it sure is.' I think he *had* taken acting lessons actually. And the man said 'Well I thought you ought to know, somebody's just completely coated it in green paint.' The cowboy said 'What!' and 'Dang my hide!' And he slammed down his glass of Tizer on the bar, stubbed out his sherbet dab in the ashtray, and stormed out into the street, and sure enough there was his horse, completely covered in green emulsion. So back he stalks into the bar and he says 'Right, which one of you nasty hornery critturs painted my horse green?' And at the end of the bar this mountain of a man, this great tough, grizzled giant gets up, walks slowly towards him and growls '*I* did! What about it?' And the cowboy says 'I just wanted to tell you, the first coat's dry.'

'You've had a terrible day!'

This is a story I told at last year's BBC Christmas party, an occasion that I remember got off to a slow start because they were still sewing the previous year's crackers together. And once again it is not entirely new. In fact this joke is so old, Samson told it, and brought the house down. Well, talking of old age, none of us is getting any younger. Many's the night I sit back wistfully and think of myself at the age of twenty-five, trying to imagine what it will be like. They say that schooldays are the happiest days, don't they? I remember the very first day I started school, when I filled all the inkwells and the teacher said to me 'Couldn't you have waited?' And I particularly remember the school dinners, especially Wednesdays, because that was my turn to carve the custard. And Fridays, when the girls had potatoes in their jackets. My goodness that really turned us on. And it was interesting the sort of thing you used to learn at school, like the fact that the girls who were the fastest cross-country runners usually came bottom in biology. Talking of sport, I see the British Sports Council has just brought out a successor to Blow Football, called To Hell with Cricket.

Incidentally, my big new movie with Steven Spielberg has been cancelled. You know, the one that combined all the thrills of *Jaws* and *Raiders of the Lost Ark*, called *Indiana Jones and the Tadpole of Doom*. But I have been making quite a lot of personal appearances up and down the country. On Sunday I was at the Savoy presenting Britt Ekland with the Queen's Award for Industry, for her work with the Youth Opportunities Programme. And I recently had the honour to be present when His Royal Highness the Prince of Wales opened the country's millionth telephone box. He made a short speech and then ceremonially kicked the glass in. Of course the privatisation of BT caused one or two problems. Millions of people rushed out to invest their savings in public telephones, and nine out of ten people couldn't get their money in.

But I digress. And back to this joke, which was actually passed on to me by my great uncle Tancred Corbett, another very small man, who worked as a steeplejack on a packet of Polos. This joke was written down in one of the many diaries he kept throughout his life. In fact he was such a fanatic about diaries, when he died they buried him in a leather jacket with a pencil down the back of his shirt.

So here is the story. There is this chap who one day overhears his little boy talking in his sleep. He's muttering 'Great Aunt Elsie . . . Great Aunt Elsie . . . Great Aunt Elsie . . .' And the next morning the man gets a phone call to say that the boy's Great Aunt Elsie has died. And he thinks to himself 'That's uncanny – but it must be pure coincidence.' Then a few nights later he creeps into the boy's bedroom again and this time the boy is muttering 'Old Uncle Sid . . . Old Uncle Sid . . . Old Uncle Sid . . .' And sure enough, the next day they hear that ninety-year-old Uncle Sid has turned up his toes. But the worst is to come. Two nights afterwards he goes by the boy's bedroom and this time the boy is muttering 'Daddy . . . Daddy . . . Daddy . . .' Well, throughout the following day the man is a nervous wreck, frightened to make any move in case it's the end of him. Terrified that at any second he's suddenly going to snuff it, or be run over by a bus, or crushed under a falling hippopotamus. Well it happens. And at the end of the day he goes home a complete shambles, and says to his wife 'You'll never believe what an absolutely terrible day

I've had.' The wife says '*You've* had a terrible day, what about me? I opened the front door this morning and found the milkman dead on the doorstep.'

Bring back the tonsillectomy!

Here is a very funny story which got big laughs when I told it last year in Las Vegas, so I'd like to tell it again tonight. And . . . I say Las Vegas, it wasn't actually *in* Las Vegas, more sort of outside Las Vegas. Islington. And incidentally I'd like to say that it hasn't changed me at all. Oh no, it would be very easy, just because I've now topped the bill at the Islington Darby and Joan Club Annual Dinner and Breakdance, to get all starry and big time. But that's not my style. I shall still be there in person next week when the Ronnie Corbett Fan Club holds its annual rally in Trafalgar Square . . . or if wet, in a diving suit.

Oh, by the way, before I go any further. I have promised to dedicate this joke tonight to our executive producer. A very distinguished and senior man here at the BBC, and tipped by some to get a car-parking space in Michael Grade's birthday honours list. My goodness, there is a man who's come a long way since he started out in this business, as a roadie for Tubby the Tuba. I remember vividly the day I first met him at the old Windmill Theatre. He was just recovering from a terrible turn. Mike and Bernie Winters. No it wasn't. In those days strip-tease dancers were his bread and butter. Till his wife caught him in the middle of a sandwich and that was that. I met him for lunch today up in the BBC's self-service canteen, where there was a bit of a hiatus. All the trays had come to a standstill due to a points-failure at Gooseberry Crumble . . . and over by the bar there was a bit of a celebration going on. In fact I think

107

some of the stage-hands had got a bit carried away, because when I arrived Selina Scott was being dusted for finger prints. Apparently the grape was flowing because one of the BBC weathermen had just become a father. The baby was said to be fine, with occasional outbreaks of drizzle later in the day.

Which reminds me, a little wave if I may to my wife and the mother of my children, in case either of them is looking in. No that's just a little joke I put in to cheer her up. My wife is rather on edge tonight because she has just finished writing her first-ever romantic novel, due to be published tomorrow. An amazing achievement really, 800 sizzling pages of love, lust and raw passion, which started out as a note to the milkman. Last night we invited a few media people round for dinner to launch it. An evening which got off to a bad start when Janet Street Porter wandered into the kitchen and the waste-disposal unit went for her. To be honest I never wanted one of those things in the first place, but my wife is *very* fussy in the kitchen. I went in there the other day and found a scarecrow in the seed cake. She is the only woman I know who puts a mud pack on a prune. However I must tell you this joke. Which is about two chaps who one day decide to have an unusual bet. And talking of unusual bets I was reminded of this joke by our local vicar, who had just been in to William Hill's to put a yankee on the Four Horsemen of the Apocalypse. And he was telling me he's been having a lot of trouble with his health just lately. He kept getting this strange burning sensation as if his nose was on fire. In the end he went to see some specialists, who examined him for three hours, and found his nose *was* on fire. So now he feels a lot easier in his mind.

When *I* went into hospital recently I had a terrible time of it. It was one of those theatres with a gallery of medical students looking on, and I was booed off halfway through the operation. To a slow hand-clap and cries of 'Bring back the tonsillectomy!' I knew I should never have gone in there because it was one of those trendy, progressive hospitals. If your child gets a saucepan stuck over his head they send round three psychiatrists with saucepans on *their* heads, to relate to the experience. And if a patient's temperature is up, a Catholic priest with a megaphone tries to talk it down.

But I digress. And we return at last to the story of the two chaps, who one day go to the cinema to see a John Wayne film. I can't remember which one, I think it was the one where he played a cowboy. And before they go in, the first chap turns to his friend and says 'Here, I bet you ten pounds that at the end of this film John Wayne falls off his horse.' And the other chap, who is not much brighter, says 'All right. And I bet you ten pounds at the end of this film John Wayne doesn't fall off his horse.' So the bet is agreed, in they go, and sure enough at the end of the film John Wayne, having cleaned up the Wild West with one hand, and anxious to get as far away as possible before Pearl and Dean come on, leaps onto his trusty steed, and splat! Falls off the horse on his face. Out come the two chaps; the first one pockets the tenner, he says 'Here. I must be honest. I've seen that film before. I *knew* he fell off his horse.' And the other chap says 'Yeh, and I've got to be honest. I've seen it before as well. But I didn't think the silly fool would do it again.'

I've always looked up to jockeys

Tonight's story is less of a joke and more a tale of personal hardship really. And that's something I've had more than my fair share of. Only last week I had a bit of a setback when I went to audition for this year's Christmas pantomime at the Civic Pallindrome, Croydon. This year they're doing a compilation of nursery rhymes and all the characters are being cast to type. The girl who plays Mary has to be contrary, and the man who plays Simon has got to be a bit simple. So you can imagine how I felt about being offered the part of Wee Willie Winkie.

However, this story is about something that happened a few years ago when I made the mistake of buying a race-horse. Because the fact is, I have always looked up to jockeys. Never down, always up. And in point of fact horse racing has been in my family for generations. It is a fact that my great great great great great grandfather actually rode in the very *first* last-ever Grand National. Like all my family he was a very small man, and very bow-legged. When he died they buried him in a banjo case. And I still go to a lot of Jockey Club functions. I remember being at a table once with Peter O'Sullevan when he looked through the menu and predicted the cheese and biscuits would come in first.

But where was I? Oh yes, last week I'd popped in to our local library, and I'd just asked the assistant to get me a couple of books down from the bottom shelf, you know, some of those health education volumes, like 'How to be a Docker and still remain active', and 'Wake up to Insomnia'. When all of a sudden I ran into my bank manager. He said 'Ronnie, I was wondering if you'd like to have dinner with my wife and me tonight.' I said 'That's very nice, of course.' He said 'Fine, we'll be round about eight-thirty.' So as it was rather short notice I sped round to our Chinese take-away, the Fo Par. It's quite good, they do a set meal of Mild Indigestion for Two, or a Quick Dash Upstairs for Four. And it was quite an interesting evening in the end, swapping old war stories. Like the time when I got my first taste of action, and was rushed to hospital with shell shock after tampering with a live Rice Crispie. Let's be honest I was such a coward in those days I once surrendered to a Marmite soldier. But it has left me with a certain sense of loyalty, and even today I can often be found sitting in a box of Action Men, entertaining the troops. Anyway, amid all our reminiscing my bank manager suddenly asked me if I wanted to buy this racehorse. Well, I thought it was worth a try, so I agreed there and then, and we tried it out in a few races, and it's fair to say that each one was a disaster. In a way you could almost read the inadequacy written all over his face, like a man who's been arrested for streaking and let off for insufficient evidence. So all this went on for a few months and at every meeting he still came in last. Well, one evening we'd got him booked in for a race at Windsor and I said 'Look, if he doesn't buck his ideas up tonight that's it. It's back to the milk round with him tomorrow. My mind is made up.' So out he goes on this two-mile race, and they're coming out onto the straight, and it's a real battle, and the jockey's lashing away with his whip, digging his heels in and generally trying to force the poor animal on. And at this point the horse looks round at him and says 'Go easy will you, mate, I've got to be up early in the morning.'

If only I'd been born a whippet

This joke has definitely seen better days, though Heaven knows when they were. Which is all rather a pity because I had hoped to do something special tonight in honour of my parents, as today is their wedding anniversary. Before I came away today my dear old father took me to one side and said 'Tipster's Lad.' It's not my fault he wanted a whippet. 'Tipster's Lad,' he said. 'It seems like only yesterday, that fateful day when your mother and I decided to start a family, and got thrown out of the cinema.' Well as beginnings go mine were pretty humble. My father in those days was an ear piercer by profession. Well not exactly an ear piercer, he was a very bad darts player. One of the first jobs he took was touring the pubs as a male stripper, but unfortunately he had very little to show for it. And he was so lazy he'd never take the dog for a walk, he used to sit it in the chair and show it travel brochures. His big problem was drink. Not only did he go out every night painting the town red, he'd go out at lunchtime to give it an undercoat. On one occasion he was picked up for making an indecent suggestion to a Belisha beacon. 'It wasn't my fault,' he said. 'Her and her friend across the road kept winking at me.' And we lived in a very polluted area of London in those days – if you tossed a coin in the air it stayed there. As a matter of fact I still suffer with my health a lot because of those days. I was at my doctor's again this week, he gave me the usual examination and said 'I'm afraid it's all in your mind, Mr Corbett, you're a hypochondriac.' I said 'I am *not* a hypochondriac, that's the one disease I haven't got.'

To cheer me up he wrote me out a joke and told me to read it three times a day after meals, so here it is. And it's an interesting story that all takes place in the jungle, and was actually told to my doctor by a man who has spent many years exploring the mouth of the Amazon. He's Shirley Williams' dentist. No he's not, that would be ridiculous. He was actually an officer from Interpol who'd tracked down this man wanted for robbery, in South America, only to be captured himself by a tribe of cannibals. Apparently by the time anyone found out, they'd eaten the detective and were just grilling the suspect.

So, here is the story. A huge, ferocious lion is one day stalking through the trees when he comes across this bunch of chimpanzees, who are casually minding their own business, drinking cups of tea, and he fixes them with a fierce glare and says 'Who's the King of the Jungle?!' Not in those words exactly. I just translated that from Lion language into English so you'd be able to understand it. Because I'm quite a linguist with animals, I once wrote a book that came out in Penguin. 'Who's the King of the Jungle?!' he says, and the chimps, who also spoke a smattering of Lion, replied as one ape 'You are, Mr Lion!' Whereupon the lion goes off satisfied, until he comes across a crocodile and asks him the same question: 'Who's the King of the Jungle?!' To which the crocodile, not wanting to end up as a lion's handbag, replies 'You are, Mr Lion!' And away goes the lion feeling rather pleased with himself. Then he comes across an elephant and again he roars 'Who's the King of the Jungle?!' At which the elephant, who is just idly whiling away the time, tickling his ivories, grabs hold of the lion with his trunk, whirls him twelve times round his head, beats him up and down on the ground, smashes him against a tree trunk and then hurls him twenty-five feet through the air into a nearby lake. Well, the lion drags himself out, battered, beaten and bruised, crawls back up to the elephant and says 'Look, there's no need to get nasty just because you don't know the answer.'

Another antique joke

Here is a rather unusual story about an antique dealer. I actually came across this story a few days ago in an old copy of *Titbits*, underneath a rather alarming report about the recent accident in which Samantha Fox was knocked down by Sandy Gall's car. An accident which wouldn't have been so serious if he hadn't gone back to run over the main points again. And on the opposite page there were some of those fascinating problems from readers, like the headmaster who had a bit of a passion for his maths mistress, and gave her a ruler as a measure of his affections. By the way I should point out I hadn't bought this magazine, I was just leafing through it in the waiting room of my local solicitor. I'd gone there because there was something of a legal wrangle going on at the time. My wife had just made a new tapioca pudding and was being sued for breach of copyright by Rentokill. And he's quite a character my solicitor. A strict Orthodox Jew who claims to have family connections dating back to Biblical times. Apparently it was one of his ancestors who was the lollipop lady at the crossing of the Red Sea. I've actually know him since I was a child, and as I'm sure I've told you before we did have a very strict upbringing when we were children. I remember once my brother and I were playing in the back garden and the woman next door was hanging out her blouse. Or very nearly anyway. And she caught us peeping and we knew straightaway there'd be trouble when our father came home. At six o'clock in he'd tramp, his face all black as

117

soot, his hair tangled and matted with coal dust. You'd think a chartered surveyor would take more trouble over his appearance, wouldn't you? And when he heard what we'd done we knew the penalty: he'd take off his belt to us, and for two hours we'd have to stand there looking at him with his trousers round his ankles until we begged for mercy.

Eventually I ran away from home and got various jobs, like teller in a piggy bank, and ring-master in a flea circus, until in the end I became the first one in our family to go into show business. That is, unless you count my cousin Berty. Three weeks earlier he'd got a key part in *The Mousetrap* and was screaming for help. He was actually an amazingly unlucky man with jobs. He once opened a dry cleaner's and it sank.

All of which has very little to do with this chap I set out to tell you about. The antique dealer. Well, one day he is lying in bed nursing an old war wound . . . I forgot to tell you, he was once a prisoner in Colditz Castle. He was involved in a daring escape plan that all went horribly wrong when a dummy of John Mills was recaptured at the French border. They're rather interesting some of these war stories aren't they? For instance, did you know that fighting conditions at Tobruk were so bad, eventually they had to call in the pools panel? Or that the British RADAR system was so unreliable the enemy had to write and let us know when they were coming?

Anyway, there he is in bed, browsing through one of his trade magazines, when he comes across this competition, which looks rather easy, so he decides to have a go. It's a sort of quiz to test your knowledge of priceless antiques. 'Name three jokes from Ronnie Corbett's act,' it says. Well this chap goes one better and names all four. And before he knew it he'd won this fantastic prize of a weekend in Paris. Well, on the first night there he meets this stunning French lady, who unfortunately doesn't speak a word of English, so he hits on the idea of communicating with her by doing little drawings on a note pad. And he starts by doing a little drawing of a cocktail glass. Immediately she seems to understand, and nods her head, and off they go to this little bar for a drink. Then he draws a picture of a restaurant, again she nods her head, and they repair to this Parisian bistro, where he draws a carafe of wine, and they have wine, and then he draws various French dishes, and they tuck into some wonderful French nosh. And in short they have a terrific evening together. Then finally the girl leans seductively across the table, takes his note pad and proceeds to do a drawing of a sumptuous-looking Louis XIV four-poster bed. Talk about lucky! But what *I* still can't understand is, how on earth did she know he was in the antiques business?

No dirty laughs, please

Tonight I'd like to reassure my regular viewers, if either of them is watching, that this week there will not be so much as a single dirty laugh from the audience here in the studio. Because this week, I'm pleased to say, the entire studio audience is made up of members of the Shepherds Bush League of Temperance and Chastity. They have all got totally pure minds and would not dream of reading anything smutty into any innocent remarks I might make. Now the other night I was lying in bed, feeling at a loose end . . . I'm sorry? What is funny about that? You are the most filthy-minded audience we have ever had in this studio, and can you please come back next week? As I was saying, I'd had a little tiff with my wife. No, she's got a very suspicious mind. Like the time she saw me in the BBC bar chatting up Sonia Lannerman, and accused me of trying to pull a fast one. That was the night there was a bit of an upset in the bar because Magnus Pyke had just ordered a round of drinks and one of his arms had come loose. It was also a special occasion for me, to be honest, because that was the evening my agent bought me a gin and tonic. Well he didn't actually buy it, he got it for me wholesale. I won't lie to you, he is something of a cheapskate, the sort of man who hangs on to the same old things for ever. There's a rumour that he once bought himself a new wallet and his jacket rejected it. And I did once discover he was not properly representing my interests on this show at all. I was going through the files in the office and found out I was being paid by the inch.

But let me tell you this joke, which I heard a few weeks ago when I went to the dentist's. I was sitting in the waiting room reading a newspaper – or was it the *Daily Star*? And my eye was caught by a little piece headed 'Don't forget to put the clocks back.' Apparently a notice for second-hand car salesmen. And it brought back memories of my first second-hand car. My goodness, old? It was the only car I've ever known with gargoyles on the radiator. And it was so badly designed the roof rack was on the inside.

Not that the one we've got now is a lot better. On a cold morning we have to kick-start the little dog in the back window. The other day my wife took it out for a spin and there was a bit of a mishap. The trouble is she doesn't understand cars, she's been known to drive into a garage and ask them to top up the ashtrays. And if I've told her once I've told her a thousand times not to put too much air in the tyres. The other day she overdid it and was last seen ballooning over Dunstable Downs.

But back to the dentist's, where at that point the young receptionist, Dental Floss, came over and said the dentist was ready for me. Now there is an old man who can be incredibly aloof – he's even got an answering machine on his hearing aid. He told me I'd got to have three fillings, and in order to put me to sleep he told me this joke, which I'll see if I can remember. One day, apparently, a chap goes for a round of golf at a rather unfamiliar course, and afterwards he's standing there in the showers, musing on his handicap, when all of a sudden he hears a group of women laughing. How I wish they were in the audience tonight. So he realises to his horror they are outside getting undressed, and that he must be in the ladies' showers by mistake. 'My God,' he thinks, 'I can't let them come in here and see my embarrassment.' So, not wanting to be recognised, he grabs up the nearest towel, wraps it round his head, and dashes out of the shower past these three women. And the women, not unnaturally, stare at him with a certain amount of surprise, thinking 'Who on earth was that?' The first one says 'Well, he's not *my* husband.' And the second one says 'He's not *my* husband.' And the third one says 'He's not even a member of the club!'

Danger: this joke can kill

Before I start tonight I've been asked to warn any young children looking in that they should not, under any circumstances, attempt to tell the joke I am going to tell tonight, as it is extremely dangerous. The audience could murder me. No, well as the father of two children myself I like to be careful. As a matter of fact my two young daughters will both be fast asleep by now. They're over there in the third row. No they're not, they're not. So I think it's safe, now, to tell you. (*He picks up a tiny box with air holes in the lid.*) I have bought them a little present – a pet. I don't want to speak too loudly because I've an idea it may be asleep. (*Rattles it about by his ear.*) Yes – it is. I actually bought this because my elder daughter has not been having a happy time of it just lately, ever since we started sending her to the John McEnroe Charm School. Where to be honest I don't think the teachers have got the first idea. The other week she had her arithmetic home-work back marked 'Twelve out of ten, must try harder.' Then for English everyone in the class had to write an essay on the subject 'How does your daddy earn a living?' And she put 'It beats me.' By contrast my other daughter is doing rather well. She's very much into music and art at the moment, and does a lot of brass band rubbings. Anyway I'll just put this box down on the floor, because you know how careful you have to be with goldfish.

As a matter of fact I've been fascinated by pets ever since the day my wife bought me a homing tortoise. It was an amazing animal actually. One day we took it all the way up to Scotland and released it. Then we jumped on the next Inter-City train home and it beat us by five minutes.

However, on to my story. This is actually a true account of a little incident that was personally witnessed by our local choir master while he was in the Oddfellow's Arms, selling copies of *Gay News*. As a matter of fact our village pub is steeped in local history. At one time it used to be known as the Shoe-maker's Arms, after a chap who lived there in the eighteenth century. The story goes that one day he joined the King's cobblers and had his needle and thread confiscated. Anyway, a few weeks ago, one Sunday lunchtime, all the regulars were there in the bar. The local farmer was just demonstrating his new idea for producing instant butter – a cow in a rocking chair – and the landlord's wife had just served up one of her extra-hot curries, and there was a mad scramble for the Pile of Pennies.

And at that point into the pub walked this rather large huntsman, with a rifle slung over his shoulder. He went straight up to the landlord and said 'Excuse me, I'm looking for a little sport.' The landlord said 'Have you tried the vicar's daughter?' The chap said 'That's no good, it's got to be deer.' He said 'Well she doesn't come cheap.' Because he has a ready wit, this landlord. The chap said 'My good man, I mean to bag some deer and I'm wondering whether there are any in that big forest down the road.' The landlord said 'Whatever you do, don't go in there. That is the private estate of Sir Hartley Ponceforth, and he has a short way with poachers. If he finds you shooting his deer he'll tie you to the back of one of his sheep.' The chap said 'What's so terrible about that?' He said 'You'll find out when the ram gets loose.' Well the huntsman, undeterred, says 'I'll take that risk.' And he departs for the forest where, as luck would have it, he bags a small deer, loads it over his shoulder, and begins strolling back to his van. Well, he's about a hundred yards from the gate when all of a sudden he is confronted by the local gamekeeper. And he thinks to himself 'Now don't panic. If I stay calm, act casual, he may not notice I'm carrying a dead deer on my shoulder.' So he doffs his cap and says 'Good morrow, sir. I've just been picking wild flowers and seem to have lost my way.' The gamekeeper says 'Don't give me that, what's that on your shoulder?' The chap says 'This? Oh – this is a rifle. You can't be too careful with all these footpads and muggers around.' At which point the gamekeeper gives him a baleful glare and says 'I'm not talking about the rifle. I'm talking about the *other* shoulder.' And the chap says 'Other shoulder, what other shoulder? (*Tries to brush it off.*) EEEEURGHHHH!!!!'

Night of naughtiness, anyone?

(*Ronnie is wearing a cheap plastic bald wig with tufts of black hair at the sides, rather like Max Wall.*)

I know what you're thinking. Where has Ronnie Corbett gone? And who is that strange gentleman sitting there in his place? Well I'm afraid Mr Corbett can't be with us tonight owing to a slight accident. Yesterday morning he was taking part in the All-Croydon 'Put a ferret down your trousers' finals, and he is still in hospital. Waiting to see if the ferret regains consciousness. No that's not true. I'll let you into a little secret. (*Removes the wig.*) It was me all along. How many of you guessed? I'll tell you why I did that. A lot of people often ask me 'What do you do when you don't want to be recognised in public?' After all, you're a show business giant, they say. Don't laugh. Oh – you weren't going to, I see. No, let's face it, as a comedian who can command a four-figure fee . . . £11.50 . . . there are times when it's nice to travel incognito. Sometimes I put this wig on, other times I wear this. (*Dons a long white beard.*) Where did he go, you're all asking. Actually I'll be honest, I've stopped wearing this beard just lately. Ever since the day I put it on, popped into our local sports shop . . . I'd just picked up a fishing rod to have a look at it, and a chap came over and said 'How much do you want for the garden gnome?'

But enough of this sophistication. If you all behave yourselves Ronnie Corbett will tell you a joke. The Zero

Option of British comedy. Well we can all do with a laugh in these troubled times. I've had some incredibly bad luck this week. On Monday I put my shirt on a clothes horse and it went lame. And as a result I've been in a bit of a state emotionally and to be honest I'm losing my ability to concentrate. On Wednesday evening I spent six hours trying to put a plug on a packet of spaghetti. But then I've always been a bit gauche in technical matters, I once saw a man milking a cow and I thought he was pulling a pint of draft Bovril. And my wife, who was sitting over at the table making a pair of curtains for the little peephole in the front door, she said to me 'Here, Ron.' Amazing memory for names. 'Here, Ron,' she said, 'why don't you go and see the BBC Doctor?' So I did. The very next day I went to see Dr Confucius Umboko. He's quite good; he practises a subtle blend of witchcraft and acupuncture. The story goes that he once stuck some needles in a Black and White Minstrel and three golliwogs died. His advice to me was to take a holiday, but to be honest I haven't properly recovered from last year's, when we went on that cruise. I could tell the voyage was ill-starred when the ship berthed at Southampton and got a parking ticket. And the catering was absolutely dreadful. The porridge was so lumpy they served it on cocktail sticks. I remember one day calling over the steward and saying 'You can send this boiled egg straight back where it came from.' He said 'I'll try, but I don't think the chicken will be very pleased.'

But I digress, because I wanted to relate this story about a monk. One which I sincerely hope will not cause any offence to any monks who happen to be watching. Well, I am reliably informed that a large number of monks listen to my jokes religiously. As a penance. So here it is. Picture if you will a little monastery and a nunnery, side by side, high up in the Spanish mountains. And down below in the valley is this rather seedy little village. You know the kind of thing, massage parlours, gambling dens, strip joints, vice rings . . . There's a lady in the front row asking directions . . . Well, one day this rather young novice monk leaves the

130

mountain and goes down into the village for provisions, loses his way, and ends up in the backstreets. So there he is, standing looking at this red light, waiting for it to change to amber, when a girl leans out of the window and shouts 'Hey, you down there with the dirty habit! Fancy a night of naughtiness for 300 pesetas?' At which the monk, not understanding her gist, takes flight down the road. And he's just turned the corner when he sees another girl standing under a lamp post, and she calls out the same thing. 'A night of naughtiness for 300 pesetas?' At which our friend runs away again, and rushes through the streets where everywhere the same cry rings out from all the doorways and alleys – 'A night of naughtiness for 300 pesetas!' Until eventually he escapes and runs back up the mountain and is in such a flap that instead of returning to the monastery he goes into the nunnery by mistake. Immediately up comes the Mother Superior and inquires what is wrong. 'Oh, Mother,' he says, 'I'm so confused, please tell me – I have to know. What is "a night of naughtiness"?' And the Mother Superior says 'Three hundred pesetas, duckie, the same as it is in the village.'

I've been asked to be brief

Tonight, I've been asked to be brief. And they don't come much briefer. Because our producer is a man who can't stand rambling. Let's be honest, our producer is a man who can't stand. Would you believe they had to put this year's Christmas party back three days, to give him a chance to sober up from *last* year's Christmas party? He is one of the few people I know who can pickle onions by breathing on them. And obsessed with gadgets . . . When he goes out of his office he leaves his swivel chair on automatic pilot. Actually, it's funny I should mention the Christmas party just like that because it was at the Christmas party that I heard the joke I'm going to tell you tonight. Once again it's not much of a joke, but then it wasn't much of a party. To give you an idea how cheapskate the BBC have become, there's now a ten per cent service charge on the coffee vending machine. As usual the party was held in Studio One, and in fact during the afternoon it had been used for *Panorama*, and they were still sweeping up after Michael Foot. He was being interviewed about that incident earlier in the day when he went to visit his new dummy at Madame Tussauds, and the dummy walked out in disgust. Now it was a bit of a dull affair, this party. After ten minutes the Britvic barrel had run dry. And as usual the BBC hadn't provided any records for the record player, so we had to dance to a dough-nut. Then all of a sudden more people turned up than expected, so they brought in their emergency plan to make the food go further: they get Big Daddy to sit on the crisps.

Incidentally, a little wave to my family, because at the moment I am in the dog-house at home. My bedroom's being redecorated. No it's not. I don't think my children were too pleased with the jigsaw puzzle I bought them for Christmas. It was a jigsaw of Botticelli's *Birth of Venus*, and we found out that if you put the pieces together a certain way it shows Robert Maxwell eating a plate of whelks.

However, I was telling you about the BBC party. Now it was all a bit quiet, to be honest. Over in the corner Percy Edwards was nesting in a bowl of twiglets, and I was just going over to him when I happened to run into my agent. He's not actually Jewish, he just hates working Saturdays. He's very fickle when it comes to religion. He belongs to this rather obscure Japanese branch of the Jehovah's Witnesses, and goes round selling digital watch-towers. And he did give me a lot of help in the early days. In fact he got me my first-ever job, as the resident MC in a confessional box. To be honest, things aren't that much better now. The other day I was booed off a speak-your-weight machine. When people book up for my act they're asked which way they want their seat to be facing.

But I digress. Here is the joke my agent sold me at the party. And it's the one about the two men who work for London Transport. That's not the joke, by the way. No, I wouldn't make any unkind jests about London Transport because, let's face it, they're doing their best to get us back on our feet. So, one night these two chaps come out of the pub, after a boisterous late night party . . . the landlord had an extension . . . which we won't dwell on. And they find their car won't start, so quick as a flash the first one says . . . or was it the second one? He says 'Why don't we go to the bus station . . . uhhhh . . . ?' Because he's not stupid this chap. Just thick. 'Duhhhh, let's go down the bus station,' he says. 'And borrow a errr . . . uhhh . . . a uhhh . . . errr . . . a bus.' I don't think they would have got too much out of *Smiley's People*, these two. So they go down to the bus depot, which is shut up for the night, and there they are in the garage trying to decide which of the buses to drive home in. And after much consideration the first one says 'Uhhh – isn't that just our luck. Look! There isn't a single 71 among the lot of them.' And the other one says 'How stupid can you get? All we've got to do is take a 92 and get off at the roundabout.'

I never had a champion conker

Before we go any further I must blow a kiss to our producer, the man who makes Boy George look like Charles Bronson, for this wonderful new chair. I think he deserves that because all the producers here at the BBC are feeling the pinch at the moment. I blame that new chap in wardrobe myself. No, times are very hard. Only this morning our conductor, Ronnie Hazlehurst, was told he'd have to cut the orchestra down. Personally I think he was wrong to string them up in the first place, but he's a hard taskmaster. Incidentally, if I seem a wee bit perkier than usual tonight, there's a very good reason. I wonder how many of you remember, five years ago on this show, I announced that I'd received a letter. Well, just to prove it was no fluke, I've had another one. Impressed? Now I know what the sceptics out there are all saying: 'I don't believe it. It's the same one as before with a dearer stamp on it.' But you're wrong. And I've brought the first letter along as well, just to show you. (*He holds up an elaborate gold frame with the letter inside it.*) Pathetic, isn't it? Why don't I grow up? If you find out, let me know, will you? No, come on, let's stop being ridiculous. My goodness, it's nothing special is it? Just a perfectly ordinary, everyday event. I've had a letter. So let's open it. (*A loud fanfare is heard, off camera.*) Thank you very much. I think we'll dispense with Black Rod. Now what does it say? 'Dear Mr Corbett. I wonder if you can cast your mind back over forty years to when you were in Class 4B at James Gillespie's Primary School. And

I wonder if you remember that little girl with the long blonde hair and big blue eyes you were once so madly in love with?' That's right! I could never get near her for her fat, spotty friend, Mabel Grimsdyke. 'Well I was her fat, spotty friend Mabel Grimsdyke.' Typical. 'Seeing you on television now I often think back to our schooldays together. Do you remember how you always used to boast that you . . . And to prove it one day behind the cycle sheds you . . .' I don't remember that. That's not true at all – I never even had a champion conker. 'PS I wonder whatever became of the old school caretaker, Mr Wogan?' No it doesn't say that. I just put that in to finish on a high note.

On very swiftly to tonight's joke, which I was reminded of a couple of months ago when I went to Australia. I'll be honest; I've never been very good at flying, which is why I always take a plane. In fact my ears pop when I wear thick socks. So I sat back and tried to read this magazine – a rather interesting article about the dying art of roof thatching, by Arthur Scargill's hairdresser. I went to Australia, incidentally, to visit my adoring public. Next year he's coming here. And I was lucky enough to be over there during the celebrations for the America's Cup yachting victory. Amazing scenes. Pictures of the team plastered everywhere. And one or two of them sober. I was very caught up in it all because I've always had the sea in my blood. As a young boy I was a stowaway on a gravy boat. I'm glad we got away for a break because back home our house is still in a bit of a state. In fact the carpets are so dirty the vacuum cleaner's developed a hernia. And we've had a lot of trouble trying to fix up my wife's car insurance. The day she passed her test Lloyds of London sounded the Lutine Bell. She is one of the few motorists who have to switch the hazard warning lights off when she stops. The other day she got a flat tyre and walked three miles to the nearest garage for a can of air.

But I digress. What I meant to tell you was that while I was in Australia I went on this day trip to a South Pacific Island, not realising it was actually inhabited by a strange race of primitive savages who worship Gloria Hunniford. I should have been more careful because it was only a few years before, on this very island, that a Gay Lib expedition ran into a group of cannibals and had to be rescued from the sweet trolley. But onward to this story I was going to tell you. Apparently there are these two Scotsmen on holiday in Italy. The Mafia have gone into hiding for a week, and naturally the chaps are after a good time. They've both drawn a blank looking for street-walkers in Venice . . . and one night they end up in this little bar in Rome, where one of them carefully consults his Italian phrase-book and then goes up to the barman and says 'Hey you, Wop-face. Gee us two pints o'draft Tartan.' Whereupon the barman, who is also a bit of a linguist, replies 'I'm-a sorry, but we no sella thees draft Tartan.' Amazing really, when you think I've never had a Cornetto in my life. So the Scotsmen reconsider and one of them says 'Well, when in Rome, we should do as the Romans do. I've got a wee idea. Tell us what that chappie the Pope drinks, and we'll have some o'that.' So the barman says 'Ah *si*. His Holiness the Pope, he is very fond of a small crème de menthe.' So the Scotsman says 'Right, in that case, gee us two pints o'draft crème de menthe.' So, to cut a long story short, they spend the night putting away tankards of crème de menthe, and the next morning wake up with an almighty hangover. The first Scotsman delicately eases himself up from under the table . . . double-glazed eyes, head like the inside of a telephone exchange . . . he turns to his friend and says 'Ahh Jeez, if that's the stuff the Pope drinks, no wonder they always carry him round in a chair!'

I haven't felt so nervous . . .

Here is a very funny joke about two American tourists. It's very, very funny. By the way I may fall asleep while I'm telling this joke. If I do, just carry on without me. I'll tell you why I say that; it's a bit of a long story, but I was up in the BBC bar this lunchtime – the producer was once again putting it away – and not before time – and he was lying there, proudly boasting to anyone who'd listen about this old banger he's got that will turn round on a sixpence. And to be honest, she does look the type. Actually I wouldn't have gone up to the bar at all but the canteen was shut again, as they were still creosoting the Ryvita. And the food in there hasn't been much to write home about recently, I'm afraid. The last time I was there I had to take the skin off the custard with a tin-opener. I was feeling, to be honest, incredibly nervous. I haven't felt so nervous since the time I found myself in the Gents with Shakin' Stevens. So I decided to go down and see the BBC nurse. As I walked in there were little yellow tablets floating all round the room, where she'd left the top off the Valium bottle. And I had a bit of a long wait because earlier in the day she'd been giving acupuncture to some wrestlers, and was now busy looking for a needle in Giant Haystacks. Anyway, she gave me some tranquillisers, so if I doze off you'll know why.

On with the joke, which is incredibly funny. Actually it's not that funny, it just seemed funny when I first heard it a few weeks ago, because I was feeling a bit depressed. It was the day every comedian dreads – I'd just got my call-up papers for *Blankety Blank*. I remember it distinctly because it was the day Mrs Thatcher announced she was planning to renegotiate the Ten Commandments. So she could have Cecil Parkinson back I suppose. Anyway, I'd gone round that day to see an old friend of mine, who I first met years ago when I worked at Butlins as an Undercoat. I used to go on and warm up for the Red Coats. And some of those audiences could be pretty tough going. The corridor with the dressing rooms in was known as Death Row. Fortunately my wife has always stood by me through all the bad times, which is amazing when you think of what she's had to put up with. Like the time on our honeymoon when I had to be given a bump start, and . . . Out!! You're making up your own jokes. We were driving round the Continent and the car broke down. I should have known better, I'd bought one of those cheap, tinny French cars, with a ring-pull sun-roof. And I'll never forget that awful boarding house we stayed in. My goodness, pokey? It was so small they cleaned the windows with Optrex. And the bedroom was so damp if you wanted to get up in the middle of the night you had to ask for shore leave.

But I digress. Back to this story, about the two American tourists. Now unfortunately we don't know their names, so for the sake of argument we'll call them Lil and Abner. Little bit of bonus information there. If you don't like the joke you can admire the improvisation. So they've come to England, and they've done all the tourist bit. They've been to Whitehall to see the Changing of the Guard, and in a London taxi to see the guarding of the change. They've fed the lions in Trafalgar Square, and they decide to round it all off they'll spend a day at the zoo. So off they go to Regent's Park to see all the animals. Well they don't see *all* the animals, because a lot of them are on flexi-time. And most of the kangaroos commute, so they have to leave early. But they see a large number of them. They see the huge Bengal tiger who only the week before ate his keeper, and is now getting visits from Lord Longford. And then suddenly the wife says 'Hey, Abner,' she says, 'I got a great idea. Let's go see the gorillas, they'll be a whole heap of fun.' So they go to the apiary, but when they get there the gorillas' cage is completely empty. They've all gone off to make a film about David Attenborough. No they haven't done that. That would be a bit ridiculous. So the woman goes and button-holes one of the keepers, who happens to be near-by, fitting a turtle with a damp course, and he says to her 'I'm sorry about this, but you've come at an awkward time of year, when the gorillas get a bit, as it were, frisky. I'm afraid they'll all be in that little den at the back there . . . doing what gorillas like to do. As you can see they've hung the "Do Not Disturb" sign on the door, and it's more than my life's worth to interrupt them.' The woman says 'Oh heck and dagnammit. And I've peeled the banana specially. We've come all the way from Schenecktady and we'd really set our hearts on taking a picture of your little old gorillas. Listen – do you think they'd come out for a bag of nuts?' And the keeper says 'Oh come on, madam, would you?'

I think the producer's just shot himself

Tonight I'd like, if I may, to relate a very funny story that I first heard when I was – (*A loud crash is heard behind him.*) I'm sorry? I think the producer's just shot himself. Plenty of time for that when we get to the joke. Now, this is a very funny story, which . . . actually there's an old adage in show business that every time you hear an unexpected bang, it means there's someone backstage who doesn't like your act. Let's hope it's not true . . . (*A long series of loud crashes ring out from behind him.*) Thank you very much for that vote of confidence. What I was going to say was that tonight I have actually been sponsored to tell a joke for charity. This means that every time I get a laugh, a pound will go to the Shepherds Bush Home for Underprivileged Studio Audiences. All right, I know what you're thinking – how will they manage on 50p? And 'There he goes again, trying to make us feel guilty for not laughing at his pathetic old jokes.' But the fact is, I do have a philanthropic side to my nature. Certain things are very close to my heart. My feet. And I've always enjoyed doing good deeds ever since I was in the Boy Scouts. To be honest I was chucked out of the Boy Scouts. I kept throwing sticks across the road and rubbing old ladies together.

Anyway, I'd like to dedicate this joke tonight to my agent, a dear friend, whose business has fallen on hard times. Once upon a time when you rang up the office you got this highly sophisticated answering machine. Now they've got a parrot that takes messages. Well let's face it, everyone's having to trim back these days. Where I live they've just opened up a self-service crematorium. And the GLC's cutbacks are beginning to bite too. Once upon a time, to dig a hole in the road, they used a pneumatic drill. Now they've got Cyril Smith on a pogo-stick. But there I go, rambling again. And to be honest I'm already in the producer's bad books this week. On Wednesday I was up in his office when Barry Manilow put his nose around the door. Not all the way around the door obviously. About half way around. And then in came the producer's secretary. A pleasant lady but not altogether with it. I once asked her for a fibre-tip and she told me to eat more prunes. She sent me in to the producer, who, to be honest, was looking a bit shaky. He'd been trying to adjust the height on his swivel chair, and screwed his head to the ceiling. He beckoned me over with his mug of starch-reduced Whitbread, and said 'Ahh, Corbett. What's all this I hear about these photos?' I knew it would get out sooner or later. The fact is, I recently posed for a set of nude photos, for *Playgirl* magazine. Under the heading 'Raunchy Ronnie – a Comic Stripped'. It's all very tasteful, actually. The nude centrefold is all quite decent. Unless you lift up the staple. The things we do for a laugh.

Anyway, he wasn't too pleased, so to keep my nose clean, tonight no rambling of any kind – straight on with the story. Picture the scene. A sleepy little village in Surrey. Nice old semi-detached house. Man in bed with the wife. Wife's husband comes home. Nothing unusual so far. Well, straightaway the wife jumps out of bed, wipes the steam off the windows, and looks outside. And down below, there is her husband, getting out of the car, carrying a dead cow on his shoulders. 'My God,' she says, 'he's come back early from the slaughterhouse and brought some work home with him.' Well it happens. I know, because I myself once worked in a slaughterhouse, the Glasgow Empire. I was in a pantomime there where the audience threw so much fruit,

Humpty Dumpty ended up as a tomato omelette. So the man, not wanting to risk sliding down the drainpipe with no clothes on, leaps across the room and hides in the wardrobe. And as he's there, crouching in the shadows, suddenly he hears this voice saying 'Coo! Isn't it dark in here!' And he looks down and there beside him is this little boy. 'Good gracious,' he says. 'How long have you been in here?' The boy says, I've seen everything, and I'm going to tell my daddy.' 'No, no, don't do that,' the chap says. 'Look if you promise to keep quiet, I'll give you a nice crisp ten pound note.' The boy says 'Certainly not. I've been brought up as a good Catholic boy, and that would be bribery. Besides, ten quid's not enough.' The chap says 'All right then, five quid.' The boy says 'Done!' A sad indictment really, of today's educational standards. So he takes the money, and he's sitting there at breakfast the next day, brandishing this fiver and his father says 'Where did you get that?' He says 'A nice gentleman gave it to me, Daddy.' The father says 'Don't lie to me, you stole it. You're a disgrace to your religion. And you know what happens to people who mock their religion, their fingers all drop off, one by one. Look at Dave Allen. Now off you go down to the church and confess.' So the boy goes down to the church, steps into the confessional box, and pulls the curtain behind him, looks around, and says 'Coo! Isn't it dark in here!' And a voice from the other side says 'Oh, no – not you again.'

Paddy, Me Boy

(*Ronnie is wearing a close fitting dark brown woollen balaclava.*)

I know what you're saying to each other: that's the first time I've seen a garden mole wearing glasses. And who left that SAS Action Man on the chair? It's pathetic isn't it, a comedian of my enormous stature . . . Do I hear sniggers of doubt? About the word comedian? No, my wife made me put it on, because I have a small cold. A small, cold what, you're all asking. No, she was very insistent that I should wrap up. Or was that the producer, I can't remember? It's fair enough, because I do seem to attract all manner of ailments and it's only a few weeks since my Hush Puppies caught distemper. And I was a very sickly child, especially with my size. As a baby I was so small I could only have one measle at a time. And sniffly noses do run in our family. So it's understandable that my wife worries, because it can get very nippy here at the BBC. This morning the producer's secretary said she was going away to get a jumper to warm her up – two hours later we found her in a broom cupboard with Daley Thompson. So my wife was very firm about it. 'Put on your woolly balaclava,' she said. 'If you take it off I will never speak to you again.' (*He takes it off.*) That's the best offer I've had all week. The fact is my wife's been very moody lately. The other night I woke up, at three in the morning, and there she was, just standing there, gazing mournfully through the window – like that.

Just gazing. She looked so sad, eventually I had to get up and let her in. I know why she's upset. We had a little tiff about how to redo our front garden. I wanted a nice lawn with all the little ornaments; she wanted crazy paving. In the end we reached a compromise and had the garden gnomes certified.

But I digress, and on to tonight's joke – which actually happened at our last end of series party. After the last show in every series the BBC throw this party up in the bar, and we'd all had a big whip-round for our old producer's leaving present, and bought him a private helicopter. I say private helicopter, it was more a sort of very primitive autogyro. Let's be honest, it was Magnus Pyke in a bucket. And as he spoke to me, the producer, a tear bedimmed his eye. 'Ronnie,' he said, 'today is the birthday of my dear old Irish mother. How I wish I could hear that song she used to sing to me as a child – *Paddy, Me Boy*. Just for old times' sake.' And it was the first time I've seen him cry since someone cracked the combination lock on his wallet. Well, I don't mind saying I was deeply touched. I was deeply touched. You see, I told you I didn't mind saying it. Because I have known our producer for many years. He plucked me from obscurity when I was still doing walk-ons for *The Magic Roundabout*. That was the time when Zebedee had been a little bit naughty, and we'd just heard that Florence was expecting a spring baby. So I went out into the corridor to have a think, and who should I see getting into the lift, but the Syd Lawrence Orchestra. So I rushed over to Syd and said 'Look, before you go home, as a favour could you play a few choruses of *Paddy, Me Boy* for our producer. It's his mother's birthday and it would mean a lot to him.' He said 'Of course, Ron,' and without further ado he and the boys all trooped into the bar and got their instruments ready. Then one of them pipes up and says 'Just a minute, *Paddy, Me Boy* – how does that one go?' And Syd says 'I don't know. I thought *you* knew it.' Whereupon it transpires that no one in the entire orchestra has heard of the song. So the producer is called over, and Syd Lawrence says to him

'Look this is very embarrassing, the band here would love to play this song your mother used to sing to you, but none of us seems to know it. *Paddy, Me Boy*. How does it go?' And the producer says 'Oh, it goes like this: Paddy, Me Boy, is that the Chatanooga Choo Choo . . .'

It's still a bit crumpled . . .

Tonight I'm a little bit excited because I've reason to believe that my new BBC pay rise has just come through. Now don't say it: 'He gets *paid* for doing that?' Well I do. To be honest, my last pay rise was nearly six years ago, when I stormed into the controller's office and demanded that they pay me what I was worth. And 37p a week doesn't go far these days. My God, it's pathetic isn't it . . . 37p a week, when you consider that the producer upstairs is earning nearly twice that. So this week, I took a militant stand, and put in a claim for a five per cent increase. And it's obviously shaken them up a bit because I've just had this top-level BBC memo delivered to me personally. Actually it's still a bit crumpled, where it was wrapped round the brick. But let's see what it says. 'From the Director General to Mr Robbie Cornett.' You see? Right from the top. At *last* I'm about to be treated with a little deference and respect, as befits my professional status. 'What's your game, Squib-face? Five per cent pay rise? I should coco, Titchy. Call yourself a comic? We could train a chimp to do what you do. If you don't like it you can lump it.' Right! Well, that does it, I'm not standing for that. I'm sorry, but as of now I am finished with the BBC, for good. And I'd like to see them replace *me* in a hurry.'

(*He exits in a huff. A pause. Then a chimpanzee wearing glasses is brought on and sits in the chair, picking its fur.*)

No, no, sorry! It was just a joke – honestly. I just went off to get a clean hanky, look. Ha ha, you can take it away now. That's the last time I buy *his* tea-bags.

So much for militancy. And on to tonight's story, which I have decided to tell as a mark of respect to my old Uncle Cyril, who was one of the great characters of show business. For twenty-five years his Widow Twanky was a legend throughout Chingford. But sadly no more. I'm afraid he's finally been summoned to that great pantomime in the sky. He's gone to work for British Airways. No he hasn't, that would be ridiculous. He's actually dead. To be honest, he was a very comical looking character, with a flat face and an incredibly big pointed nose, and now he's dead they're going to use his head as a sundial. And it's interesting, because his brother, my late Uncle Horace, was also in panto, and spent forty years playing Humpty Dumpty. I remember his cremation was held up for nearly an hour while someone went to fetch an egg-timer. When I think of it, it's been quite a year for bad news. Last Sunday, there we all were at home, taking things easy. My little nephew was sitting on the carpet, playing with his Tonka . . . and my wife was upstairs in our daughter's play room, trying to smoke a double-glazing salesman out of the Wendy House. Well, I'd just settled down after breakfast with the *News of the World*, reading a thrusting, in-depth theological dissertation about a vicar who was caught on the church roof with an Avon Lady. 'Ding-dong Merrily on High' it was headed. And suddenly we heard that the chap next door had just been rushed to hospital. It was very tragic because he was a businessman who was very big in kitchen equipment, until his accident. He fell on top of a Kenwood Blender and liquidated his assets.

But I'm wandering again. So on with this story, which concerns a little old lady who has just lost her husband. And she decides that for some companionship she'll buy herself a pet. Well, we all like pets don't we, as long as they're not chimpanzees? I remember when I was a boy, we were so poor I used to have very cheap pets. For my seventh birthday my parents bought me a semi-detached tortoise. And my father couldn't afford a homing pigeon, he had a budgie on elastic. So she buys this dog, and every afternoon at teatime, regular as clockwork she takes him for a walk down to the newsagents for her evening paper. Well, one day, many years later, she is getting rather frail, and has just pulled a hamstring filling in her football pools, so she gives the dog the money for the newspaper, and she says 'Now, you're sure you don't mind going on your own today?' And the dog says 'No, I don't mind.' There we are, a talking dog. Already the joke has got novelty value. That's about all it has got. And off he waddles down the road with the money in his mouth. Well, four hours go by and there is no sign of him. 'My God,' she thinks. 'Perhaps he's been kidnapped, or got tangled up in a toilet roll somewhere.' So she throws on her hat and coat and begins combing the streets. And eventually she passes this dingy alleyway and there to her horror is her little dog, with a little lady dog, having a good time among the dustbins. So she grabs a nearby bucket of water, throws it over them and says 'Well! I've never seen you do *that* before!' And the dog looks at her and says 'Well, I've never had the money before.'

To which God replies . . .

Tonight I have made a solemn binding pledge to our
producer to get straight on with the story, and not
indulge in any of my customary rambling. So here goes.
There is this priest. Well let's face it, it only wastes time, if I
just sit here and whitter on about everything under the sun.
It's pointless, it's irrelevant and there's no need for it. So
tonight, right on with the story. Which as I say is about a
priest who one day decides to become a missionary. Added
to which, we have just got a new controller here at the BBC
and he is very hot on efficiency. My goodness, is he ever
efficient! Not very often, no. But he is better than the last
controller. He stepped down recently with the highest
redundancy settlement ever paid out by the BBC – £400
and a *Crackerjack* pencil. Not that he will need it, because
his wife is something very big in the City. The Thames
Flood Barrier. No she isn't. That was just a case of mis-
taken identity when she went for an early morning dip. No,
he actually started here as a producer with children's
television in 1956; and I remember that year because at the
time I was having a torrid affair with one of the Wooden-
tops, and he was kind enough to pull a few strings for me.
When he left, the BBC threw one of their special parties in
his honour. The usual thing – bottles of champagne,
Scotch, gin, vodka, were all locked away for the night and a
can of 7-Up was opened. It was a bit of a lively evening –
just as they were about to hold the raffle for the Twiglets
a fight broke out between two of the guests. Rather

unfortunate, because Marcel Marceau was being strangled by the Invisible Man, and everyone just stood around and clapped. That was the night – it's all coming back to me now – when I leapt onto the dance floor and did my rather racy impression of John Travolta. I suppose it must have been the animal in me. I had a ferret down my trousers.

But where was I? Oh yes – no rambling. Mustn't upset the new controller. Because this new controller thinks I am the funniest man in Britain. He's been told to stay in bed and take things easy for a while. So on with the joke. Once again it's a bit of an old joke, so if you feel like joining in with the words . . . Don't. And as I say it concerns this priest, who one day decides to go on a missionary expedition to Africa. And he's a bit jittery in case it turns out to be dangerous, so he prays to God. He says 'Look, as a devout Christian I am a firm believer in life after death – I support Luton Town . . . but if it's all the same with you, I'd rather not get killed, because I'm not sure how it will affect my social life.' To which God replies 'Don't worry, I will look after you. All I ask is that you trust me – no matter what happens, trust me and I will look after you.' Quite a good impression that, wasn't it? So off goes the priest and a month later there he is, trekking across Africa to his mission station on the back of this donkey. He was meant to go on an elephant but at the last minute it did the dirty on him. And ran away! Don't make up your own stories, please. And just as they're starting to climb up the mountainside, all of a sudden there is this mighty avalanche and the priest goes hurtling down the mountain again, and ends up clinging precariously by his fingernails to a wafer-thin precipice, while down below in the swirling waters there is this monstrous crocodile snapping away. Now don't ask me why a crocodile was taking photographs, I don't know. Perhaps it was a Japanese tourist. Now at this point a small single-seater aeroplane happens to be passing overhead and the pilot looks down and says 'Excuse me, sir. I can't help noticing that you are clinging precariously by your fingernails to a wafer-thin precipice. Is everything all right?' Remembering what he's been told, the priest steels himself and bravely replies 'Yes, I have put my trust in God and He will protect me.' And the plane flies away. Later on some natives are paddling up the river in a boat and one of them stops and asks if he needs any help, and again the priest replies 'No, I have put my faith in God. He will look after me.' And away they go. An hour later a helicopter whirls overhead, and naturally the chap inside leans out and calls down. 'Can I interest you in a Barratts Home at all?' he says. No he doesn't say anything of the sort. He asks the priest if he's in trouble, and once again the priest, still sustained by his faith, replies 'No, I have put my faith in God and I know that He will look after me.' At which point he falls off the ledge and is eaten by the crocodile. The next thing he knows he's walking round Heaven and he meets God. 'This is terrible,' he says. 'You said if I put my faith in you you'd look after me. What went wrong?' And God says 'Well I don't know, I sent a plane, a boat and a helicopter for you . . .'

You can't expect wit

Tonight I have a rather sad announcement to make. This will probably be the last time I'll ever sit in this chair and tell you a joke. (*Tumultuous applause and cheers.*) No, please. You're upset, it's understandable. But try and hold back the tears. There's a woman down here opening a bottle of champagne. No it had to happen sooner or later. At long last I have been lured to Hollywood. I'm delighted to say that Paramount Pictures have bought up the movie rights to my sensational autobiography, *The Ronnie Corbett Story*, filmed in Microscope. It's all very exciting and I've got the draft screenplay here, look. 'The Ronnie Corbett Story, starring Burt Lancaster as Ronnie Corbett.' A challenging role if ever there was one. He'll probably end up getting an Oscar. 'And co-starring Ronnie Corbett as the Oscar.' There are some stunning scenes in this film I don't mind telling you. How about this for an opening. 'Scene One. The Workhouse. Ronnie Corbett has just been born. His thin, waif-like mother picks up the infant Corbett in her trembling hands and holds him out towards the midwife . . . "Please, Miss, can I have some more?" Scene Two. Fagin teaches Corbett to steal jokes.' No, I have to admit the plot has been slightly romanticised. The real story isn't nearly as cheerful. The first house we lived in was so damp, we held a housewarming and it boiled away. That is the strange thing about reading a script of your life story. It brings back so many memories. Like the day my wife and I got married. Well we didn't actually get married, she won me in a pass the parcel. It happened at one of those big show-biz bashes. It was very late in the evening and all the guests had got a bit merry on Henry Cooper's knockout punch. The cabaret that night was a bit rough – a string quartet of BBC cleaning ladies, playing Air on a J-Cloth. And Rod Stewart was doing some close harmony numbers with a dodgy starter motor. And then someone said 'Let's play pass the parcel,' and before I knew it I was being tossed round the room, and every time the music stopped the person left holding me peeled something off. I'll never forget my wife's words as she removed the final piece of wrapping. 'Oh look, just what I've always wanted – a bendy toy.' I wasn't embarrassed, because I've always been very proud of what nature has given me. Little things please little minds I suppose.

However, on to tonight's story. And I must apologise if it doesn't seem all that funny, but it was told to me by the BBC's Director General, so you can't expect wit. Thursday morning I received the invitation into his office, and as usual I had to wait a few minutes while they finished blow-drying the flock wallpaper. And then I went in. 'Ah, is that you down there, Corbett,' he said. 'I thought I saw a movement in the carpet. Come and sit yourself down, Sweetie.' He calls me Sweetie. It dates back to when we first met and I was sleeping rough in a bag of jelly babies. 'I've got an awfully funny story,' he said, 'which I thought you could do in your piece of nonsense this week.' So, for better or worse, here it is. And apparently this is a story that actually happened a few weeks ago when our controller was over in New York. He was staying in one of these incredibly swish skyscraper hotels. Elevators with in-flight movies, a Jehovah's Witness in every bedside cupboard . . . and central heating that is very exclusive. If you fancy a sudden blast of hot air you just press a button and Russell Grant comes up and reads your fortune.

Anyway, one night the D-G was sitting in the lounge having a drink when he noticed a little scene between two men at the bar. One of them was an Oriental gentleman, the other a Jewish ice-cream manufacturer, who worked on sundaes. Well, as the Oriental gentleman is leaning across the bar he accidentally knocks over the Jewish gentleman's drink, and he immediately gets very upset. 'My life!' he says. 'First Pearl Harbour. Now this. That's just the sort of thing I'd expect from your people.' The Oriental gentleman says 'Pardon me, but I happen to be Chinese, and it was the Japanese that bombed Pearl Harbour.' The chap says 'Chinese, Japanese, what's in a name?' And promptly picks up a nearby soda syphon and squirts it all down the Chinaman's shirt. 'Typical!' shouts the Chinaman. 'Well, that's just the sort of thing I'd expect from *your* people. First you sink the Titanic, now this.' The Jewish chap says 'Sink the Titanic? What are you talking about? That was nothing to do with the Jews, that was an iceberg.' The Chinaman says 'Iceberg, Goldberg, what's in a name?'

'Sing us a song, Yehudi!'

Tonight I've had a special request from a lady in Bromley . . . so I want to be away early if you don't mind. But before I go I've got something exciting to show you. Just to fill you in on the background, I was chatting to the producer the other day, after one of our weekly rugger matches. I forgot to tell you, I was recently elected captain of the BBC rugby team. I won't pretend we're a great side – last week we lost at home to the Beverly Sisters. But we do try. And he came up to me afterwards in the showers to compliment me on my tackle. He gave me a playful wink with his frosted glass eye – he's a bit of an introvert – and he said 'Ronnie, Luvvikins . . .' To be honest, he's been a bit on edge just lately, ever since he heard there was a big strapping convict on the loose in his part of London. He took it very seriously, and had his front door fitted with a daisy chain. 'Ronnikins,' he said, 'I just thought you'd like to know that the BBC have finally agreed to give you a new set on the show.' Well, it cheered up my wife, who was feeling a bit down at the time. The night before we held a dinner party, which was slightly marred when my Aunty Ethel shot herself during a game of Happy Families. I was heartbroken I can tell you. I only wanted Mr Snip The Vasectomist for a full set. Anyway, the top and bottom of it is that the BBC's top scenery designers have been working right into the early hours of the afternoon to come up with a swish new setting for my chat spot. And this is the result. (*He unveils a small model of an elegant set with chairs and a bar.*) The brand new Ronnie Corbett set. Impressed? Now I know what you must be thinking – isn't it a bit small, even for him? No, no, this is not the actual set, this is just a model of it. Even the BBC aren't that stupid. Even they wouldn't think I could actually work in a set this size. (*A miniature phone rings in the set. He answers it.*) Hello? What? Oh really? (*Puts it down.*) So much for that. Another dream shattered. Actually, to be honest that's not so very different from the house I lived in when I first got married. That was so small, when we left they demolished it with a conker.

But I digress. On with the story, which was told to me by our musical director, Ronnie Hazlehurst, who is not actually in the studio at the moment – he's upstairs hosing the orchestra down with soda. And it's a musical story which concerns the great classical violinist, Yehudi Menuhin, who one night arrives for a concert at the Royal Festival Hall, Bingley. Not the greatest venue in the world, but let's be honest, live entertainment is becoming a thing of the past these days. Even as I speak there are plans before the GLC to pull down Bernard Manning and build an amusement centre. I know what it's like to get lumbered with some dodgy bookings. I've never gotten over that Far East tour I did a few years back, when I went to Polynesia. I was appearing under my Pidgin English name, Short Feller Belong Knackers Yard. And I well recall the night I was booked to perform in front of a tribe of cannibals. The manager showed me to my dressing room and I saw it had three stars on the door. I said 'Does this mean I'm top of the bill?' He said 'No, it means you'll keep for two months in a frozen food compartment.'

Anyway, there is Mr Menuhin, getting ready for the big concert. The entire London Philharmonic are up there on the stage – they would have been in the pit, but it had just been closed down by Ian McGregor. And as they strike up the intro, out walks the great maestro to take his bow. And as he does, the audience all rise as one man. Let's be honest, the audience *was* one man. To his utter dismay Mr Menuhin looks across the footlights, and sees that the entire theatre is empty except for this one podgy little man in a flat cap and bicycle clips sitting in the back row rolling himself a black pudding. Well, he is absolutely speechless. 'I am absolutely speechless,' he says. There you are, I told you he was absolutely speechless. 'I cannot possibly give a recital under these circumstances.' To which the chap replies 'Oh, no you don't,' he says. 'I'm not budging till you've done your turn. Now get a pigging move on, you great wally.' No you're wrong, it wasn't Richard Baker. Well, again Mr Menuhin is adamant. 'I must reiterate that I cannot perform to an audience of one man.' The chap says 'All right, I'll tell you what, Yehudi. Just sing us one song, then I'll go.' Well, this is the final insult, but Mr Menuhin is so desperate to get rid of him he'll do anything, so he swallows his pride and proceeds to go into a rather feeble rendition of the only song he knows, *Show Me the Way to go Home*. And when he's finished the chap gets up and looks at him, he says 'Well. If that's the way you sing no wonder the bloody place is empty.'

The Lichfield Look

It gives me a tremendous thrill to announce that my new LP *Ronnie Corbett Live at the Salvation Army Soup Kitchen* – Croydon's premier night spot – has just gone Tupperware. We haven't had all the figures in yet, but early estimates from record shops up and down the country suggest that sales of my new album may already have topped six copies. Completely shattering my previous record. Which is something else people have been doing. A remarkable success story when you consider that this new LP isn't even out yet. It will actually be released tomorrow. The man who produced it will be released next week. And no expense has been spared; they have even commissioned Patrick Lichfield to take a special photo of me for the cover. Naturally I had a few reservations because he does have a tendency to flatter his subjects and make people look more glamorous than they really are. But I said I don't want any of that on *my* photo. Just show me exactly as I really am, and I'm pleased to say that's what he's done.

(*Ronnie holds up the record sleeve, which is a photo of Robert Redford wearing black glasses, and the title as above supered over it.*)

Now be honest, he's definitely caught me, don't you think? Do I hear sniggers of derision? No, this record is rather special to me because it contains all the funniest jokes I've told in thirty years of show business. Unfortunately when they put the hole in the middle it disappeared. Incidentally, I shall be giving away a free copy of this record to everyone who laughs at my story tonight. Everyone who doesn't laugh will get two free copies. So you've been warned.

Now this story was told to me the other night in the pub by our local Catholic priest, who'd just popped in to give the last rites to the bitter. The landlady was just about to give me my usual, then her husband walked in and that put paid to that. It was a bit of an eventful evening actually. At one point there was total panic and the whole pub had to be evacuated, after a tip-off that someone had planted a Max Bygraves single in the juke box, added to which the local MP had had a bit of a skinful, and ended up losing his seat in the Gents – traditionally a Labour stronghold. Anyway, I got chatting to our priest, who is actually a big improve-ment on the old priest, who left recently under rather embarrassing circumstances. He was not only defrocked, but had his earrings and handbag confiscated. This new priest has a much more commercial approach. He was the one who introduced the drive-in confessional box, and his latest gimmick, the Senior Citizens Super Saver. If you're over sixty-five you can sin anywhere in Britain at weekends for only five Hail Marys. Anyway, while we were chatting he told me this very funny story about a young lady who goes to America. Which is rather a coincidence because earlier this year I went on a safari holiday to Kenya. I say safari holiday. It was actually one of those cheap, very fast sight-seeing tours, where they strap you to the back of an ostrich and fire a gun. Next year I have sworn to take my car when I go away, because I have just bought one of those new Anglo-Jewish cars, the Austin Schmostin. Hand built by rabbis. It's got all the gadgets, if you forget to fasten your seat belt, a little voice comes on and says 'Kill yourself! I should worry.' But back to the young lady, who decides she will get to America by stowing away on a boat. So she promptly goes to the docks and secretes herself inside a crate of herrings. The box is loaded onto the ship and two hours later she's off. And so would you be inside a crate of herrings. Well, we pick up the story again a fortnight later. The girl has just been discovered and is marched into the captain, who says 'Do you mean to tell me you've been stowed away on this ship for two whole weeks? Where have you been all this time?' The girl says 'Well, you may as well know the truth. On my first day here the second officer found me, and took me along to his cabin. And every day for the last fortnight he has let me hide there. He's given me hot meals, let me use his bath and shower, and very generously let me sleep in his bed.' 'I see,' says the captain. 'And was that *all* he did?' At which the girl takes on a crimson hue, she says 'Well . . . I must admit, he has been taking advantage of me.' The captain says 'I'll say he's been taking advantage of you. This is the Liverpool to Birkenhead ferry.'

I was Dolly Parton's chiropodist

Thank you very much Ronnie Corbett fans everywhere. But mainly nowhere. Now, since the last series, when I read out a letter from an old school chum, thousands of you have rung up, asking me to talk a bit more about my schooldays. I say thousands . . . hundreds of you have rung up asking me to talk about my schooldays. Let's be honest, nobody has rung up asking me to talk about my schooldays. It's strange, isn't it, that when people do call you on the phone, it's always at the most inconvenient moment. Like last week, for instance, when I'd gone out of the house for the day, and someone rang up the answering machine while it was in the bath. And it was actually a very important call because we'd just heard that our eldest daughter, after three years of trying, has finally managed to get into Oxford. I told her to stay off that bloody ring road, but she wouldn't listen. Now, you may ask, why am I telling you all this? I seem to have wandered off the point somewhat. I was going to talk about my schooldays. And to add a touch of authenticity I have brought this along – one of my old school reports. 'St Crippen's Comprehensive, annual report. R. G. Corbett, vice captain, Wimpey House.' No, I think it can be very illuminating, to look back and see how you actually did at school. I mean here I am today, an international sex symbol . . . No, I am. I've just finished shooting my new blockbuster feature film, *Rocky Three and a Half* . . . I only appear briefly in the film, as Dolly Parton's chiropodist, so I was working in the dark to a large extent. So let's see what I was like at some of my old subjects. 'Maths: pathetic. Science: awful. History: abysmal. Geography: dire.' This can't be right, I'm sure there was one subject I was good at. 'English: his knowledge of vocabulary is lamentably deficient.' Ah yes, that was it. I knew I was good at English. I always remember English; I used to sit next to Herbert Wibley the school sneak. He had a nasty habit of snipping through people's conker strings when they weren't looking. Grew up to become a vet if I remember rightly. 'Music: sluggish progress. It has taken a year to stop him blowing the xylophone. When he sings in the choir, has to be fitted with a mute.' No, it is true that I was a bit of a terror at school. I'll never forget the day we put itching powder in the gym mistress's bed, and watched the headmaster scratching himself all through assembly next morning. 'Religious Knowledge: ignorant and lazy. When told to find Joshua in the Book of Numbers he rang up directory inquiries.' Right, that's enough of that.

And by a strange coincidence it actually reminds me of a joke which I was going to tell you, which has a rather religious flavour, and concerns the vicar of a little parish church which is slowly falling into disrepair. The vicar is at his wit's end, and one morning he's sitting there at breakfast; he turns to his housekeeper and says 'Bless my soul.' Because he's a bit of a do-it-yourself addict. 'Bless my soul,' he says. 'The place is a shambles. The roof is falling to bits – I've seen death watch beetles in there wearing safety helmets. What am I to do?' And his housekeeper, who is just hoovering the cornflakes, looks up and says 'Well, you know what I think, Reverend, the building is possessed by an evil, diabolical force.' He says 'No, we paid off the loan to the Abbey National months ago. The whole thing is in need of restoration, and unfortunately the clerical coffers are bare.' 'Well,' says his housekeeper, 'in that case there's only one solution. I will have to sell my body on the streets.' At which news the vicar spits out his mouthful of fruit juice, accidentally baptising the cat, and says 'You'll do what? You – an employee of the parish vicar? Plying yourself in the village as a bit of rough trade? What happens if the bishop finds out?' She says 'He'll have to pay the full rate, the same as everybody else.' So to cut a long story short, off she goes that very night, and a few hours later she's back, opens her purse on the table; she says 'There we are. That's not bad for a night's work. Twenty-five pounds and ten pence.' The vicar says 'Twenty-five pounds and ten pence? No, that *isn't* bad. But tell me, who on earth gave you ten pence?' And she says 'Everybody.'

Cynics may scoff

Thank you very much and welcome to Ronnie Corbett's World of Comedy. I know – it's a small world, isn't it? Cynics may scoff, but I am actually held in very high esteem within this company. Here at the BBC I am placed on a pedestal. So they can see where the voice is coming from I suppose. But that is the really great thing about working for the BBC, the feeling of status they give you. The total respect with which they treat your work, the deep feeling of reverance and admiration, and . . . (*A shabby cleaner in overalls goes past him with a vacuum cleaner, shaking ash over him as he goes*.) Let's be honest, they don't give a monkey's. You think I've got problems – that was the Controller of BBC 1.

Anyway, here is a very funny joke, about a Scotsman. And by the way, a little wave to my own relatives up in Scotland, because we have just had another sad death in the family, I'm afraid. My great Uncle Willie, who was a local bus driver for thirty-five years. At his funeral we had to wait forty-seven minutes for the coffin, then three came at once. The funeral was in a very remote area, the local branch of Express Dairies was a cow on a skateboard. I remember all the members of my family vividly – my young cousin Gloria, who went to London in search of a sugar daddy, and came back with a jelly baby . . . and my old grandad. He was a local miner, and as he got older could only stay underground for very short periods at a time. They had to lower him down the pit on a yo-yo. Some of those miners were incredibly militant. They wouldn't pick their noses without a productivity bonus for face work. Of course in his early days my grandad was a famous explorer in India. Out of a party of twenty people he was the only one who managed to get over the rapids. I blame all that curry myself.

But back to the joke, which my agent picked up for me while he was in Bournemouth watching the Krankies. Now why he was at the SDP annual conference I don't know, but he was. He is actually a very remarkable man, my agent, and very careful with money. As a child he taught his piggy bank to sit up and beg. In his younger days he used to manage the Dagenham Girl Pipers, now he can only manage one or two of them. But where was I? I was just going to tell you about last week, when I was out in the garden, ascending the north face of the rockery . . . I'll be honest, our front lawn has not been much to look at lately, since five of our garden gnomes took early retirement. And my wife had just finished unloading twenty-five sheets of glass from the back of our car; she said to me 'Don't you think it's time we found a window cleaner who makes house calls?' I know why she was a bit tetchy. It was that two-week holiday in America. It didn't agree with her at all, she was moody and miserable the entire fortnight. Next time I'll have to take her with me I suppose. The reason I went to America was that I was taking part in the finals of the Mr Universe contest. I know that sounds hard to believe, because I am not what is generally thought of as an American beefcake. More a Scottish shortcake. But this was the Little Mr Universe contest. All the entrants have to pose on a catwalk in skimpy bathing trunks while the judges decide which one has got the biggest muscles. I came third after a recount. They found out one of them was a goose pimple.

But I digress. Here is tonight's joke, which is about a little Scottish chap who goes on a train to Falkirk to stay with relations for Hogmanay. So at ten-thirty he boards a sleeper . . . she complains to the guard and he's thrown off the train. Well he boards the next one, and very soon he's sitting there minding his own business, when the door to the compartment slides open and in comes the inspector to check the Scotsman's ticket. Which he duly produces. 'Just a minute,' says the inspector, 'this ticket's out of date.' 'Out of date?' exclaims the Scots chappie. 'What are you talking about? I paid tuppence three-farthings for that ticket and it's only been used once. I ironed it specially this morning. It's as good as new I tell you!' The inspector says 'Come on, you can't travel on that – come up with the money you crabby old skinflint.' Well, at the mention of the word money the Scotsman comes over all faint, he says 'Och aye, you cannae do this to me, I'm not a well man . . .' Well, the guard is not impressed by this pathetic piece of acting. I'm not that impressed with it myself to be honest. And immediately he snatches up the Scotsman's suitcase and opens the window. He says 'Now then, you tight-fisted old scrooge, pay up now or I'm throwing this out of the window.' The Scotsman says 'My God! That's a typical Sassenach trick. First you try and rob me of all my money, and now you want to kill my only son!'

Did I say Bridlington?

(*As Ronnie speaks we see a huge packing case beside his chair.*)

Here is a rather amusing story about a chap who goes to live in Bridlington. By the way, take no notice of this. I'm sorry it's here, but there's nothing we can do about it. That's the BBC for you. You'd think they'd at least sweep the floor before I came on, wouldn't you? This would never have happened under our old producer, before he was put on the transfer list to *Match of the Day*. Now *he* has been having a few marital problems apparently. Since he's been out covering soccer matches he hasn't scored at home all season. Anyway, this joke concerns a . . . Oh this is pathetic. As a matter of fact I did lodge a formal complaint about it just before the show with the head of light entertainment. And I must say that his reply – 'Naff off you four-eyed little plonker' – did leave something to be desired. I said 'Look, the audience out there don't want to see some ugly great eyesore on the screen.' He said 'I know – that's why we've put a packing case in front of you. Don't forget,' he said, 'your BBC contract expires this week. So if I were you I'd watch my step, Lofty.' Well, I am not standing for this sort of cavalier treatment, I want to know what's inside this damned thing anyway. I mean, what if my contract does expire? They always renew it. That is the one good thing, at least, about being a comedian. It's one job where they can't replace you with a machine. (*He opens the*

181

crate to reveal an automated Ronnie Corbett robot, which whirrs into life.) I'm sorry, what is this? This is some sort of joke, surely.

Machine: Good evening, it's wonderful to be with you, isn't it Ronnie? In a packed programme tonight we'll meet a man who crossed a table tennis ball with an extremely tall chamber pot and got a ping-pong piddle high po.

Oh for goodness sake, don't encourage it! This is technology gone mad – get off – out! The idea. That a machine like that can do anything I can do. I wouldn't mind, but my wife's just ordered one.

But enough of this sophisticated repartee, and on to tonight's joke. Now I'm hoping this joke will cheer everyone up because we're still a bit depressed here about that incident at lunchtime, when the BBC's lift operator was sunbathing on top of the building. He fell off the roof and then suddenly stopped between the third and fourth floor. What with that, and a tip-off that an Animal Rights group has laced a bottle of rat poison with some BBC coffee, it's all been a bit fraught. Now once again I have to admit this joke is not exactly original. In fact I was reminded of it the other day while browsing through a copy of the *Snail Fancier's Gazette*, which I have started taking, ever since I bought myself a racing snail. I won't pretend it's fast. It's a bit slow over the fences, but I'm really devoted to that snail. Every weekend I'm underneath it, tinkering away . . . Well, we never had decent pets when I was young, as I've said before. You have to remember I was brought up in a very tough neighbourhood. My father used to ride shotgun on a Tesco's supermarket trolley. I remember we used to live in constant terror of the local Gay Mafia, run by the Fairy Godfather. If you refused to pay protection, a couple of the boys would come round and criticise your curtains.

However, that has nothing to do with this joke I was going to tell you, which is about a man who moves to Bridlington. And I must just give a little wave at this point to my wife, because it was actually in Bridlington that we first met, Anne and I. She was working on the beach at the time, on the donkey rides, and it was love at first sight. In fact she was so overcome she nearly dropped the donkey. But back to the plot. The chap who has just moved to Basildon. Did I say Bridlington? It could have been either. But since this man has just got a job with Essex County Council it's probably best to make it Basildon. Rather than Bridlington. It doesn't bloody matter where it is, to be honest. The main thing is that one day he is looking out of the window when he sees, coming up the road, a little old man carrying two enormous heavy boxes, one in each hand. And as he watches, the old man struggles up the road with the boxes, puffing and panting, and disappears round the corner. Two hours later he looks out and there comes the old man again, still gasping for breath, doubled up with these enormous boxes. Well, this happens every day. Every time he looks out, there is this man lugging these two massive boxes about. Then one day the chap happens to bump into the old man; he says 'Excuse me, you wouldn't have the time on you would you?' And the old man puts the boxes down, mops his brow, and looks at his watch. He says 'Yes, it's 12.15. In Nairobi it's quarter past three, and in Guatemala it's a quarter past six. Lighting up time in Tibet is 3.37 a.m., the temperature in Rangoon is 83 Celsius, the FT Index is up 6.2, ICI has put on twenty-five, and Elizabeth Taylor has lost two and a half pounds since Friday. In New Delhi England are 205 for six, with Gatting on seventy-one, the 10.37 from Clapham to Bromley is running nine and a half minutes late, and Sainsbury's pork sausages have just gone on special offer in Aberdeen at 57p a pound.' The chap says 'That is incredible. That is the most amazing watch I have ever seen in my life.' And the old man says 'I know, but carrying these damned batteries around is *killing* me!'

We'll ignore the booing from the Royal Box

(Across the foot of the screen is a narrow strip which reads 'HM Government Warning: This Man's Jokes Can Damage Your Health'.)

Thank you very much for that spontaneous applause, and we'll ignore the booing from the Royal Box. It's not my fault she couldn't get tickets for *Crackerjack*. Now, tonight some of you may have noticed a slight addition to the picture on your screens. And I'd better explain, this is due to a new law, the TV Viewers Protection Act, brackets, Comedians of Limited Growth, which makes it compulsory for all comedians under five foot, with big black glasses, who sit in chairs telling jokes, to carry a government health warning. And it's fair enough I suppose, because research does show that the stories I tell can lead to fatal illness. People get sick to death of them. Now to be honest I've been a bit off colour myself just lately and my imagination's been playing tricks on me. The other day I was in the garden, trimming the big cockerel on the front hedge, and as I picked up the shears I'll swear I heard it say 'Not too much off the top please.' And I must admit my new car has been a bit of a disappointment – the Robin Reliant Turbo – not the fastest car I've ever driven, in fact the warranty ran out while I was backing it out of the showroom. All in all it's been rather a tragic week. Last Thursday morning our little

185

pet sausage dog, Ronnie Junior, died, and rigor mortis set in. My wife took it surprisingly well. Within half an hour she'd plucked up the courage to lay it out on the kitchen table, and by lunchtime she was rolling pastry with it. She's a bit absent-minded, I'll be honest; I once asked her to let the cat out, and she was up all night with a needle and thread. To cheer her up I took her to Madame Tussaud's for the unveiling of the new wax effigy of Nigel Lawson. It was so realistic, at one point his head fell off and the pound rose twenty-five cents against the dollar.

But on with the joke. Which I am bound by law to tell you was best before August 3rd 1876. And which I last heard quite a few years ago now, when I was doing a very cheap Christmas show in Chinatown, called *Jack and the Beansprout*. It wasn't much of a part, I was appearing with Dudley Moore and Charlie Drake as a pantomime earwig. And I must make a good job of this story tonight because I am not in the BBC's good books ever since I disgraced myself over their new suggestion box. I suggested they put a hole in the top. The next day I was summoned to the managing director's plush office on the seventh floor. My goodness – big? I've seen a fly paper in there with the Red Arrows stuck to it. And he does take a very keen personal interest in this show. Every week he and the director get together upstairs and kick a few ideas around. Then they come down here and kick me around. And when I saw him this week he was feeling rather full of himself, showing off his new Lacoste nose job, with the little crocodile over one nostril. 'Get a bleeding move on in that chair tonight,' he said. With uncharacteristic eloquence.

So tonight for the first time in history I shall dispense with any rambling and get right on with the story, which is the one about the policeman, who is out on his beat one night in the middle of winter. It's five below zero, he's got icicles round his helmet, goose pimples on his truncheon, and he's trudging around the streets. Not much action about – he's cautioned a couple of cockroaches for kerb crawling, but otherwise all is quiet. And as he's standing there on the corner, little white flakes start to flutter down from the sky. And immediately he snaps into his police training. 'Hello, hello, hello,' he says. 'Little white flakes – fluttering down from the sky – it must be snowing. My God,' he thinks, 'the forecast said three feet of snow and I've only got two boots on. I'll freeze to death. I knew I should have worn my big police overcoat.' So to cut a long story not very short he hurries back to his house, only to find his wife has gone to bed and bolted the door. He throws a pebble up at the window, and out pops his wife's head. She says 'What do you mean by getting me out of bed at three in the morning? Go away or I'll call the police.' He says 'Look, I'm sorry to wake you, dearest, but if you'll just throw down my big police overcoat I'll be on my way.' So she disappears from the window, gets the coat, throws it down, and away he goes, warm at last. Five hours later he's back at the nick, walks into the mess room, and says 'My God. What a night that was. Thank goodness for the old police overcoat, it's saved my bacon.' His mate says 'Yes, you can say that again.' Then he gives him a rather strange look, he says 'Here by the way, George – how long have you been a sergeant?'

And now a serious note

I'd like to begin tonight, if I may, on a rather serious note. It's something of a sensitive subject, but one I hope we can all approach in an adult, and mature fashion. The question of my sex appeal. And why it didn't bring in a single donation. Now I knew you wouldn't take that seriously, but the fact is, it's a popular fallacy that men of my diminutive stature don't make great lovers . . . as I pointed out in my recent book on the subject *How to make a little go a long way* – in which I recounted my first ever awakening to the attractions of the opposite sex. At the age of twelve, it was. I can still remember it vividly. I'd just climbed half way up Carmen Miranda, and suddenly I lost all interest in scrumping her apples. A risky venture in those days because I went to a very strict school. I remember, the boy who sat next to me was shot for hurrying a Murraymint.

Anyway, what I thought I would do tonight was to select completely at random a letter from one of my adoring female fans, and see what it says. 'To the most erotic man on TV. Care of *The Two Ronnies*.' See what I mean? I get this all the time. Let's see what's inside it. 'Dearest Ronnie, you are the sexiest hunk of man I have ever seen. Virile and masculine, yet warm and sensuous. Last night I dreamt that you and I were ... How I long for us to make mad, passionate music together, Ronnie. Say it can be so. All I ask is that you get rid of that weedy little drip who's on the show with you, and we can . . . Perhaps while he's spouting

his usual drivel in that chair we could slip away together and
. . .' I might have known it was too good to be true. 'PS
Please ask him to tell the joke about the American tourist
and the Red Indian.'

Which brings us neatly, if not very convincingly, to
tonight's story. Now I'm glad it's this story actually, because it should cheer up my family, who are all rather upset
tonight, as today holds rather painful memories for us at
home. Because it was exactly a year ago today that that
terrible incident occurred, when I was kidnapped. I haven't
talked about this before in public, because it's left a lot of
scars, naturally. But it all happened one Saturday afternoon. We were taking part in a big charity event on
Wimbledon Common, in aid of an unfortunate chap on
Come Dancing who'd been blown up by a land mine during
the military two-step. It was very flattering because my wife
and I were the guests of honour, and as a special tribute, the
first night of our honeymoon was being re-enacted by the
Sealed Knot Society. I'll admit the catering left a lot to be
desired. It was in the hands of the BBC's Canteen man-
ageress, and I'll swear she doesn't read her own recipes
carefully enough. On this occasion she served up a lemming
meringue. Every time you went to eat some it kept throwing itself off the table. Now, it was 5.30, I'd just left to go
home, when suddenly without warning the kidnappers
struck. A car roared up alongside me, the door was flung
open, they asked me if I'd like a nice bag of sweeties, and I
got in and we drove off. We drove for three hours till we
came to a deserted, disused old building which they'd
obviously picked because no one would ever go there.
Watford Football Ground. No it wasn't. I shouldn't be
unfair to Watford because they're doing their best to make
a go of things. Only this week they signed up two new
spectators. So anyway, the kidnappers sent a note to the
BBC which said 'How would you like to see Ronnie
Corbett strung up on a meat-hook?' The next day they got a
letter back from the head of variety, saying 'This shows
promise, let's have lunch.' So eventually they issued an

ultimatum. If the BBC didn't leave £5,000 in a hollow tree on St Pancras Station *immediately*, within twenty-four hours, I would never be seen alive again. Eleven months went by. It went through various BBC committees, the ransom note was read out on *Points of View*, and the kidnappers got fed up waiting and let me go, alive and unharmed. And the BBC sued them for breach of contract.

However, that is all past fortunately, and so on with the story about the American tourist, who is on a package tour, going round the United States. And the tour takes them deep into Indian Country, down through Wounded Knee to Twisted Ankle, finally arriving at Athlete's Foot, where they all pile out of the coach and the guide draws their attention to a wizened old Red Indian who is standing by the side of the road. He says 'That over there is Leaping Turtle, last of the Navahos. And he has the most amazing memory of any man alive. Who'd like to test him out?' So this chap steps forward, he says 'Tell me, Leaping, can you recall what you had for breakfast on February 25th 1947?' And without any hesitation the Indian replies 'Eggs.' The chap says 'Well I'll be plum tuckered, that's incredible.' At which point their time is up, and away they go again. Well, the chap enjoys the trip so much that twenty-five years later he does it again. And sure enough, there standing by the same roadside is the same Red Indian. A bit older now obviously . . . splashing his scalps with Grecian 2000, delivering a rather limp war cry . . . I forgot to tell you, he was in the Salvation Army. And the chap can't believe it. 'That's amazing,' he says. 'Leaping Turtle – still alive after all these years.' And he goes up to him and says 'How!' And the Indian looks round and he says 'Scrambled.'

For sale: one chair

A rather nostalgic moment tonight, because after fifteen years it looks as though the time has finally come to say goodbye to the old chair. Owing to mounting financial pressure the BBC is having to sell off many of its prize assets. As from next week I'm to be rehoused in Dave Allen's ashtray. And by the way, for anyone who doubts that the BBC are in deadly earnest, I've got here the official estate agent's blurb for this chair. Listen to this. 'Ronnie Corbett's Chair, Television Centre, W12. We are pleased to offer this much sought after little property, nestling in the idyllic surroundings of Studio Eight's Scenery Dock. Situated within easy walking distance of the floor, and just a stone's throw away from Terry Wogan. Brackets, stones not provided. Comprises one sitting tenant, of the mature pre-war type, with ample scope for extension downstairs.' How dare they! 'NB Jokes in need of some modernisation. Realistically priced at twenty-nine and a half thousand, but we'll take ten quid.' No, I can tell you I intend to fight this through the courts. And I'm quite confident because I have got a very good lawyer, who can work miracles. He was the one who got me compensation for unfair dismissal from the Harlem Globetrotters, so he's hot stuff. Actually, talking of lawyers reminds me there are still one or two legal hitches over my new autobiography, *Secrets of a Super Stud – Rambo Ronnie Reveals All*. At long last I have decided to kiss and tell, because I think it's time people saw the other Ronnie Corbett for a change. Ronnie Corbett the Swinger.

You may scoff, but many's the night I can be glimpsed mixing with the jet set down at Tramp, in my tight, clinging jeans, with my big gold medallion, my duffle coat open to the navel. Bopping away till three, sometimes four minutes past seven at night. I'll admit it hasn't always been like that. I haven't always been as physical with the ladies as I am today. I was the first man to take advantage of Slumberland's Emergency Relay Service. And I was quite a late developer emotionally. I used to have this dream that I was alone in a dressing room with five topless dancers, playing this little piggy went to market. I suppose it all stems from being a very small child. When I was born my mother demanded a recount.

But as I say, we are having some legal trouble over one controversial passage in my new book, about the time I spent the night in Britt Ekland's bedroom, and got arrested for loitering in a public place. So if it fails to appear you'll know why. But on to tonight's story which is a true-life tale that actually happened to some very close friends of mine. And since it's a bit personal I'd be obliged if you didn't let it go any further. Now, they are a bit of a strange couple, I'll be honest. Every so often they invite us round for dinner, to their chic little pad in Hampstead. All very open-plan, they've just had the goldfish bowl and the budgie's cage knocked into one. And a very exclusive neighbourhood. Where they live they don't have morning papers – Alastair Burnet comes round and shouts through the letter box. Anyway, here we come to the interesting part, and not before time. For twenty-five years the husband has kept a big wooden trunk at the foot of the bed, and he has made his wife swear a binding oath on her grandmother's grave – which is not easy because she was buried at sea – that she will not, under any circumstances, try and open it. And being a loyal wife – and an idiot – she keeps her word. Until one day, it's their wedding anniversary, and she comes downstairs expecting to find something on the breakfast table – a card, or some flowers or something. But there's nothing. Not a sausage. So she thinks – well there is *one* sausage. And a couple of fried eggs and some toast, but no presents. So after he's gone to work she thinks 'Right, just for that I'm going to open that damned trunk upstairs and see what *is* inside it, once and for all.' Which she does, and when she opens it, inside she finds four golf balls and £800 tied up in an elastic band. What can it possibly mean, she wonders? Well, that night her husband comes home, full of remorse, loaded with flowers, boxes of chocolates, a bucket of Chanel Number Five, he says 'How can you ever forgive me? Happy anniversary my petal.' At which his wife is deeply moved and says 'I have a confession to make. You know that crowbar I use to get the skin off the rice puddings? Well, while you were out I used it to open that trunk upstairs. And I know what's inside – four golf balls and £800.' 'Oh my God,' says the husband. 'Well there's nothing for it now but to come clean. You see, throughout our marriage, every time I've been unfaithful to you I've opened that trunk and put a golf ball inside. So now you know.' 'Oh dear,' she says. 'I see. Still I suppose four golf balls in twenty-five years – that's not *so* bad. But tell me, what about the £800?' He says 'Well, every time I got a dozen together, I sold them.'

STEWART BOYLE AND JOHN ARDILL

THE GREENHOUSE EFFECT

THE GREENHOUSE EFFECT: without it the world would freeze but now it's causing rapid overheating and climate change. Why? What is it? What causes it? What will its effects be now and in the long-term? Why are 'ozone-friendly' labels on aerosols and fridges both good news and bad news? Why will cutting down the Amazonian rainforest affect the temperature in Manchester and Melbourne? How can car fumes and cattle ranching influence the weather? And why do artificial fertilisers threaten the polar icecaps?

Stewart Boyle, Energy and Environment Programme Director of the Association for the Conservation of Energy, and John Ardill, environmental correspondent for *The Guardian*, have written THE GREENHOUSE EFFECT – a practical guide for the non-expert which will answer all your questions about the most serious environmental problem we have ever faced, and provide a range of solutions.

POST A LITTLE HAPPINESS

Post·A·Book

A Royal Mail service in association with the Book Marketing Council & The Booksellers Association.
Post·A·Book is a Post Office trademark.

RONNIE BARKER

IT'S HELLO – FROM HIM

When, a little while ago, Ronnie Barker decided to retire, he just left a message on his answer phone. No Positively Final Appearance, no press statement, no fuss.

After nearly forty years, a 'jobbing actor', in his own phrase, was leaving the stage. Farewell Norman Stanley Fletcher, goodbye Piggy Malone, Arkwright, Clarence...

The end of a career that began in 1948 when a seventeen-year-old bank clerk handed in his notice. He was off to join the Manchester Repertory Company, based for obscure reasons in Aylesbury.

'You're mad,' said the bank manager. 'Stay five or six years and you could be a cashier.'

Instead he, and the rest of us, had to settle for a stage, film and TV career as a brilliant comic actor – and writer. A very professional, well-liked man who made us laugh and laugh.

Bank managers do make mistakes.

'Wonderfully entertaining'
The Sunday Times

'His own good humour shines through on every page'
The Stage

'Ronnie Barker's love of life and wonderful sense of humour is clear throughout the book'
Newcastle Journal

RICHARD MCBRIEN AND ROGER PLANER

HOW TO GIVE UP SEX

Essential reading for the over-sexed.

You enjoy sex, you're good at it, people like having sex with you – at least that's what they've always told you.

Now, suddenly the sexual revolution is over. You know the time has come to give up sex, but can you shake off the habits of a lifetime?

The good news is that you've probably been practising celibacy for years without even knowing it. Every time you stopped having sex, even if only for a few minutes, you were in fact being celibate.

This frank and uninhibited new book helps you build on those minutes, showing how to make your sex life a lot more disappointing. In commonsense, down-to-earth language it answers the questions you were too afraid to ask, such as 'How often should I be celibate?' and 'Can I be celibate with two people at the same time?'

Explicitly illustrated throughout, with a dozen new celibate positions, *How to Give Up Sex* is the first comprehensive guide to not having sex and the perfect introduction to the secret joys of celibacy.

HODDER AND STOUGHTON PAPERBACKS

PAMELA DES BARRES

I'M WITH THE BAND

I'm with the Band is for everyone who remembers when *Rolling Stone* was essential reading. When Jim Morrison was still a living affront to decent civilised values and the Joshua tree meant Gram Parsons, not U2.

I'm with the Band is the story of Pamela Ann Miller who left her Valley high school and her squeaky-teen dreams of Paul McCartney to become Miss Pamela of the GTOs, part of the Zappa family, groupie, grievous angel, sweetheart of the rodeo and L.A. woman.

Chris Hillman, Jimmy Page, Keith Moon, Waylon Jennings, Mick Jagger, Captain Beefheart, Robert Plant. All these and more (Howie) were friends, confidants, lovers . . . For those were the days when groupies were stars in their own right and Cynthia Plaster Caster's hand-raised collection was greeted with open-mouthed awe.

Miss Pamela who had fun, fun, fun and Californian heartache and weird, wonderful times – and has written it all down with a wicked wit, great attention to detail and the highest of high spirits.

'The brightest, sexiest and funniest of the lot'
New York Times

HODDER AND STOUGHTON PAPERBACKS

MICHAEL CAINE

MICHAEL CAINE'S MOVING PICTURE SHOW

Britain's own Oscar-winning superstar takes the lid off the movies in this hilarious and revealing bookful of fascinating facts and outrageous out-takes . . .

In their 1953 movie *Abbott and Costello Go to Mars* Bud and Lou actually end up on Venus!

Oscar Levant claimed he'd known Doris Day *before* she became a virgin!

Sophia Loren's mother once won a Greta Garbo look-alike competition . . . but when Charlie Chaplin entered a Charlie Chaplin lookalike contest he came third!

Winston Churchill worked as a scriptwriter for London Films in 1934 and Edward VIII is the only British monarch ever to have acted in a screen drama . . .

NOW, NOT MANY PEOPLE KNOW THAT

HODDER AND STOUGHTON PAPERBACKS

MICHAEL CAINE

NOT MANY PEOPLE KNOW THAT!

An Almanac of Amazing Information

Royalties to the National Playing Fields Association

- Fred Astaire's first screen-test notes read: 'Can't act, can't sing. Can dance a little'
- The original title for the bestselling book GONE WITH THE WIND was BA! BA! BLACK SHEEP
- Karl Marx disapproved of Engels' mistress because she was too common
- Only human beings sleep on their backs

Not many people know that!

A feast of fascinating trivia and invaluable information from Britain's best-loved actor. Michael Caine casts light on the most bizarre and remarkable facts and feats of every subject under the sun – all of which are true.

HODDER AND STOUGHTON PAPERBACKS

ANDREW MORTON

DUCHESS

Her Royal Highness the Duchess of York. The woman the world knows as 'Fergie' is the most talked about member of the royal family in years. But beneath her controversial public image what is the red-haired Duchess really like?

Royal writer Andrew Morton has followed the Andrew and Fergie romance from the start. Now he has written the first full biography of this thoroughly modern woman whose energy, warmth and zest for life have changed the face of the royal family. "The Duchess will set the tone and style of the House of Windsor in the 21st century."

'Crammed with Fergie facts . . . Morton is one of the royal family's favourite reporters and his witty, chatty, slightly cutting edge contrasts favourably with the usual honeyed royal prose.'

Woman's Journal

'Meticulously researched, it is peppered with new facts'

Today

HODDER AND STOUGHTON PAPERBACKS

PILAR WAYNE

MY LIFE WITH THE DUKE

John Wayne. The Duke. The big man standing tall and dominant in his films and in life. A legend around the world, in himself and in his work he embodied America. He knew it and he was proud of it.

Stagecoach, *Red River*, *Rio Bravo*, *The Alamo*, *True Grit*: not just a list of films but a roll call of honour.

And like all truly great men, stories were told of him: some true, some false, some silly but affectionate.

Pilar Wayne lived with the big man for twenty-five years. Wife and mother, she knew him like no one else could. Through the good times and the bad times, the wild times and the quiet, sad times, she was there. Now, eight years after he lost his last heroic battle, when the hurt has died down, when the invent-all, tell-all scandal-mongers have had their say, she has written *her* story. The story that only Pilar Wayne could tell: the truth about the man behind the myth . . .

'Packed with anecdotes and insight'

Photoplay

HODDER AND STOUGHTON PAPERBACKS

MORE TITLES AVAILABLE FROM
HODDER AND STOUGHTON PAPERBACKS

☐	508137	**RONNIE BARKER** It's Hello From Him	£2.99
☐	49473 X	**RICHARD MCBRIEN & ROGER PLANER** How to Give Up Sex	£2.50
☐	50637 1	**PAMELA DES BARRES** I'm With The Band	£3.50
☐	50827 2	**MICHAEL CAINE** Michael Caine's Moving Picture Show	£2.99
☐	50638 X	**STEWART BOYLE & JOHN ARDILL** The Greenhouse Effect	£3.50

All these books are available at your local bookshop or news-agent, or can be ordered direct from the publisher. Just tick the titles you want and fill in the form below.

Prices and availability subject to change without notice.

HODDER AND STOUGHTON PAPERBACKS, P.O. Box 11, Falmouth, Cornwall.

Please send cheque or postal order, and allow the following for postage and packing:

U.K. – 55p for one book, plus 22p for the second book, and 14p for each additional book ordered up to a £1.75 maximum.

B.F.P.O. and EIRE – 55p for the first book, plus 22p for the second book, and 14p per copy for the next 7 books, 8p per book thereafter.

OTHER OVERSEAS CUSTOMERS – £1.00 for the first book, plus 25p per copy for each additional book.

Name ....

Address ....

....